TINY LITTLE BOXES

HOW TO COPE WITH **EXISTENTIAL DREAD** BY WAY OF **ICE CREAM** AND OTHER MEANS

CHRISTINA DYLAG

NIHILIST ICE CREAM

TINY LITTLE BOXES
*How to Cope with Existential Dread by Way
of Ice Cream and Other Means*

ISBN 978-1-5445-0823-8 *Hardcover*
       978-1-5445-0822-1 *Paperback*
       978-1-5445-0821-4 *Ebook*

This book is dedicated to my family, of blood or energy, in this physical plane and outside of it. We're only here for a time.

Na Zdrowie.

CONTENTS

C A V E A T...9

WHY AM(ARE) I(YOU) R E A D I N G THIS?......................................11

THE F I L T E R..15

A LESSON IN L A N G U A G E..19

SO W H Y DOES IT M A T T E R ?...27

SEPARATION AND D U A L I T Y...35

NARRATIVES IN C O L O R..49

N A R R A T I V E S EXTENDED...55

Y O U VERSUS THE O T H E R...75

OUR "MAKE IT" S T R A T E G I E S..85

L E N S E S IN ACTION..89

EVERYTHING IS E N E R G Y..93

"PROOF" AND THE EXISTENCE OF A HIGHER B E I N G............................99

MORE ON G O D (OR WHOMEVER) AND OUR LANGUAGE BARRIERS.....................101

A WORD ON P E R C E P T I O N...109

WE ARE A L L INTERCONNECTED...113

I N T E R C O N N E C T E D N E S S AND A HEALTHY SOCIETY.................119

L A R G E R SYSTEMS AT PLAY...123

RELIGIOUS D I V E R S I T Y. BORN N BRED, BABY............................131

NURTURING YOUR T A L E N T S..135

CHEAP I M I T A T I O N S...147

THE SLIPPERY E G O..155

M O R E ON NARRATIVES...159

CONTROVERSY AND DISTORTED O N E N E S S...................................165

S Y S T E M S...173

MORE ON R E L I G I O N. SAME SAME BUT DIFF...............................177

CULTS, RELIGION, I N S A N I T Y...185

PLATO, KANT, MULTIPLE INVENTION, E T C...................................199

S I M I L A R I T I E S IN PHILOSOPHY AND RELIGIOUS THOUGHT (+ NIETZSCHE)..205

A N E W NIHILISM...209

HOW TO EMBRACE W H O L E N E S S AS AN INDIVIDUAL.........................217

PSYCHOLOGICAL E G O I S M AT WORK...221

T R A N S C E N D THE BULLSHIT...225

WHAT ABOUT M E (Y O U)??...231

OUR I L L U S O R Y VIEW OF LIFE...235

WE'RE ALL CARTOONS IN A CARTOON WORLD....................................239

R E D I S C O V E R Y...243

WE DON'T KNOW MUCH OF A N Y T H I N G....................................247

SELF-W O R T H...251

SEEING THE FLAWS IN O T H E R S / SEEING THE FLAWS IN O U R S E L V E S....259

INFORMAL A B S O L U T I O N AND DEVISING MY D R E A M...................267

EXISTENTIAL D R E A D...289

ACKNOWLEDGMENTS...291

CAVEAT

Hi there.

For a somewhat expected initiation, I might start by offering my name. It's Christina. Often confused as ChristinE for whatever reason. Could be a subtle nudge for the elimination of the arguably needless third syllable; the suggestion being a consequence of secretive expense reports re: time spent pronouncing first names. Wouldn't necessarily explain the flawed email greetings but yeah, probably just realistically a strange coincidence. O r i s i t ? ?

I'm less likely to resort to an explanation in the trusty vein of c o i n c i d e n c e, because I don't particularly subscribe to the belief of such things. In fact, I don't really believe in much at all—not in an entirely cataclysmic 666 blacksoul-death expression, but more in line with the abandonment of the body of "truth" suspended in air-tight buoyancy before our oily cherubic faces. every day. since birth. What I *do* believe is often up for debate (via internal dialogue or otherwise), which makes for a lively discussion, albeit an inconclusive saga most times, especially if done strictly within the confines of my own Anton Chigurh-leaning mind: thoughts being a bolt stunner with altogether disprovable facts playing victim. You can sense the struggle I'm sure.

Why?

bc nothing is truly knowable.

&

the human experience is entirely subjective.

Whatever follows in these pages reflects what I t h i n k I know now based on my own experience and my run-in with thought and knowledge that existed before me. Meaning: it is in no way absolute truth, but *m y* truth *for n o w*. The unraveled square knot. In that way, it is only prescriptive if you want it to be.

So, yes. Now that that's clear:

WHY AM(ARE) I(YOU) READING THIS?

I'm not sure about you but for me, occupying the role of architect in my own life tends to feel burdensome at times. *I figured out that I like ice cream, what else do you want from me?* vibes. The influx of familial advice care-packages, paired with Instagram spiritual affirmations a la Deepak, serial killer podcasts, the k-hole deep dive into YouTube makeup tutorials, linked with the sudden(?) emergence of collagen as unorthodox but *eh, fine* superhero of our generation... at least one half of it... at least the outer layer... It all sort of clouds the brain with this grey, numbing film. A metaphorical one, no less.

Have you ever watched Supermarket Sweep? Contestants race through the store, scouring the aisles past Captain Crunch voyeurs in hopeful Olympian fashion for the most sought-after, wallet-annihilating items. The winner is the most predatory capitalist, I guess. Anyway, that's what life's all about! Grab'n'Go. The American Cream.

You've successfully incorporated your exercise regimen (even if that means circulating your hand to mouth in rapid succession), career and/or life objectives, blood brothers and transient acquaintances, healthy but also splurge-heavy diet, a significant other (or the clear-skied freedom of singledom), and an arsenal of moisturizers that all collectively promise to transmute your facial skin into celestial silk babies. If not currently acquired, trying to do so.

But then you're also acutely aware that the earth is on its last leg, with our ecosystems declining into an abysmal soup of despair, so you hesitate to toss that confetti too frequently, right? I mean, not only does confetti lack sustainability, but the celebratory element borders on evolutionary faux pas.

It's hard to divvy up your own energetic pie chart: How much should I embrace the ineffable beauty of this lifetime, and how much should I mourn? Wow, this charcoal-lavender ice cream is somehow life altering in a mystical but also convincingly privileged way, and, also, children are locked in cages within my own alleged "First World" country, so...

What I would like to attempt to do here is give you permission to live. To expand. To do whatever it is that you think you're supposed to be doing. We're all making it up as we go, and any rule or regulation or nip slip from our governmental powers that indicates something counter to that is, well, damn wrong. You heard it. You read it. S c o o p it up.

Choose your own adventure. irl.

We are at a critical step in our human evolution on this planet. Dash over the railroad tracks and continue on, or linger atop hot-rolled steel and await the inevitable.

Spirituality and the emergence of a newly awakened state continues to make its way to the forefront as a result of merging cultures, the culmination of experience, and the advancements of technologies that have allowed for increased and improved travel and communication.

Humans have always done the trial-and-error approach to life, attempting to uncover the truth behind what constitutes food versus poison, how to nurture the body and keep all organs from perishing, how to construct a dwelling, or explore the earth, or decode the male brain. With every generation, the informational pool expands and we're better apt to not only teach one another about our findings, but grow collectively toward a fresh, vast understanding that encompasses all of this knowledge. It's not a luxury to be able to delve into the deeper aspects of our psyche and beyond, but a privilege.

Philosophers have dealt with these questions for centuries. Existential quandaries, in tandem with a spiritual crux, have infiltrated the far corners of society all the way into the big daddy breadwinners like organized religion and the keepers of the moral code. Now, spirituality and the access point to enlightenment take shape in more than just a word (God/Allah/Universe/Vishnu/Starbucks) and the associated dues. Language falls away to make room for something more inclusive and uninhibited. If you are or were anything like me, verbiage surrounding spiritual and moral principles was at best, questionable, and at worst, divisive.

Our energetic being, our soul, our metaphysical self emerges in grander, fuller fashion, and this embodiment of spirit remains accessible to everyone. It's digestible and consumable. Still, though, there is a palpable severance between the spiritual world and the "realist" world, and I can say with authority that I have been a member of both, which is why I wanted to write this thing: a bridge, ready and able, linking the two. Spirituality and the essence of existence can, will, and do exist in myriad forms. The magic dwells in the movement of the body, with such things as yoga, sports, walking, and purely being; it flourishes in music and in architecture; it lives and breathes literally in every known sphere of knowledge and area of interest. It exists in everything. Ya gotta tap into it. Brush up against that counter window and choose. Taste. Dig your teeth right in.

THE FILTER

From the beginning of our individual lifetime, we see the world through a very specific and consistent lens, the portal of human engagement, like rose- or mauve- or sepia-toned glasses. We know no other way of being, as if the glasses are plastered to our little nugget heads. It is who we are (or, rather, who we think we are) and what we process and perceive. It is only through this lens that we are able to experience the complexities of life, which take on the identity of things that bring us enjoyment (frozen delicacies, Keanu Reeves, Golden Retriever puppies), and things that make us suffer (erectile dysfunction commercials, period cramps, political movements dictated by the Kardashians). We learn to navigate the world and dodge the bullets of suffering through the various coping mechanisms we've developed over time.

Throughout our early days of life, there is no other way to process this external stimuli. We have to make sense of the world before we look beyond it. You are thrust into a world in which you are the perceiver and the rest of the physical elements are "the other," outside of you. We interact with our community and its actors and, in turn, we react and respond, giving credence to the belief that the world is the cause of our inner emotional environment.

From birth, our mother is our creator and the person or entity with the capability to cease our pain. We are hungry and she feeds us. We are upset and she coddles us. We are annoying and she bathes us in Elmos. If she denies us, we are left feeling abandoned and without love. It is through this relationship (and/or other relationships of a similar nature) that the cycle of "you" and "the other" commences. We forget (mostly because we do not possess the developed mental faculties) that we were once one with our mother, our c r e a t o r. For the entirety of life going forward, any instance in which "you" are separate from "your creator," pain or suffering takes hold. To embrace the oneness of our original state of being (one with our mother/our creator) is to love. Whenever we act in accordance with the oneness, we are acting in love, and whenever we create further separation and honor the illusion of "you" and "the other," we create a snowball effect of the same, creating more suffering for us and for the other(s).

The caregiver-child relationship is the microcosmic representation of the larger scope of existence: the part to the whole; singularity as a distinct, inseparable component of wholeness. As much as they appear to be separate, they are infinitely linked.

As a little baby person, we learn that our pain can be either alleviated or heightened by the presence of our mother, our parents, or our caregivers. And in the absence of human touch, we are granted access to toys, or treats, or phones. This is the beginning of our disjointed relationship with the world, and the belief that all of suffering and joy can only be found outside of ourselves. It is almost as if joy and suffering are done to us. It is not wrong or disgraceful, it merely *is.* There is no other way for the undeveloped mind to process the world, and, thereafter, it is how we learn to manage within our physicality.

There is no specific time in life when we are told, *This is all an illusion. You are actually the only one in control of your hurt and joy.* Even if that supposed time did happen, we wouldn't believe it, because for all of life we have known that happiness could only exist outside of ourselves. We create our emotional harmony and we create our suffering:

Like that time you let the coffeehouse barista's attitude about alternative milk options throw you off. Or when the purple PT Cruiser couldn't figure out how to disengage his turn signal, which, you know, made you inexplicably upset. In all instances of suffering, *we choose* how to respond. How mad we'll be. How we really feel about it. And yet, we attempt to pass the buck on that one, calling into question the external world versus our internal dialogue about it.

Much undoing needs to happen in order to fully collapse the veil.

Over time, we learn catch-all phrases that are designed to undo the suffering: *just be happy, live in love, don't sweat the small stuff,* and countless other phrases and religious-centric jargon that are mostly lost in translation. We hear these phrases forever in succession and yet fail to grasp the true meaning within them, because words, like all things that appear within the physical world, are a cheap replacement for the e s s e n c e beyond them. Words can only point to the truth, but it's in our individual and collective power to *live in it.*

Step 1

Realize that you are presently (and have always been) inextricably linked to the rest of existence in a meaningful way. Part to the whole, baby. Also realize that the external world is not the controller of your mental, spiritual, and emotional well-being. Give up that ghost.

A LESSON IN LANGUAGE

All of life is a systematic doing and undoing; a within and without; a learning and an unlearning; trust and distrust; a give and take; ebb and flow. We learn within this dichotomy. You wouldn't know pain without the absence of joy, and you wouldn't know the full o n e n e s s of creation if it weren't for the separation. It is necessary and absolutely essential to operate within the duality in order to fully grasp the truth beyond it (at least within the realm of humanity). For this reason, it is not wrong or unsavory to embrace the physical world. It is and it exists within our scope of understanding. Is it wrong to see a beautiful bird as a distinct entity outside of our human body? Of course not. But to know and fully grasp that both the bird and the human are, at the very core, not only the same, but interconnected... that's the sweet spot. That good good. All of existence and the systems that work within it point to the essential truth of oneness. We're all one, my brother! I didn't say it. Science did. We're all pure energy at the crux. It is only when we recognize the unity in life, that is, the interconnected nature of all things, that we are able to experience life in a complete way, full of unconditional love.

From birth, our caregivers attempt to make the world palatable to us. The only modality to do so is through language.

A parent lifts up an object and exclaims the name of said object. The parent holds an apple up and says, "apple." "Aaaa-paaaal." Over time, the child accepts that this object is an apple. The child is praised for understanding the truth of apple and what apple is. The nugget brain learns that this apple is something called food, which enters the mouth and feeds us. Food is good and apple is good for you. It is not banana. It is not dog.

Many humans throughout time and from the knowledge of the first apple, accepted the subjective truth that the smooth-skinned red item was an apple. Sometimes apple is red or green, or even yellow, but never blue. So many people accepted this word in connection with the apple, that if someone were to declare that the apple was actually called a byler, it would be comical or false, at the very least. This person would be insane, according to all other humans in agreement for apple. *You know this is actually an apple, stop pretending,* the others would think. It is, in fact, so common-place and simplistic in terms of relative understanding that very few people would believe that this person doesn't actually know what an apple is. *Everyone knows what an apple is.*

The relationship between the seemingly innate properties of the apple and our relative understanding of it can then be applied to all other aspects of life. We are so deeply entrenched in our perspective of the world and its properties that we are unable to see beyond it.

Our understanding of the apple is entirely based on our relationship to it. Apple is food because we, as humans, can eat it for energy. We only know apple through our very specific viewpoint. Its use for us gives it weight. To other species, apple may be poison, danger, or an insignificant object.

The "truth" of the word apple in accordance with the object is not wrong, necessarily, but it grossly undermines the essence of the apple. We need the word apple in order to make sense of it in the world and communicate its importance to others. If not its importance, at least its individuality in the world. Words and characterizations are the only way in which we can see our place and purpose in the physical world. Words are the only way that I can communicate these thoughts to you, and yet these words fail to fully explain the essence that lies beyond them. All words do. Everything that appears to us in the physical world is a distortion of the essence of being. This essence — its oneness, its nothingness, its enormity and capture of both everything and nothing — cannot be transcribed. All physical elements in the physical world only point to this t r u t h. They beg us to look beyond them.

When we look at the example of the apple, we must also look at the other examples that occur within our scope of understanding. The more exposure we have to certain "truths," the more evident they appear. Making sense of the world and operating within it, armed with impenetrable truths, gives us relative comfort. Our parents gave us praise when we accepted certain notions (apple) in our early life, and we continued to find acceptance through the process and understanding of all other forms of life. It is comfort, but an impermanent pacifier.

The more we relate to the world in an acceptable, widely-known and believed way, the more we can enmesh ourselves within the fabric of all humanity. Or so we think. What we don't know, is the more we latch onto the physical world, the less we are able to see past it and connect with the true spirit of existence, experience the freedom of orchestrating meaning without big brother on the nanny cam.

Our understanding of the object "apple" morphs over time to encapsulate much more than its original meaning. "Apple" as food slowly shape-shifts into an item that represents health and vitality. If I eat it, I too am healthy (as an extension: a valuable member of society). If I am seen with it, I am viewed as either fit (or trying to be) or a teacher with grossly unimaginative pupils. Maybe the image of the apple resurrects strong biblical allegory and associated Sunday School PTSD. The more time we have here on earth, the more integrated we are in the complex structures of language and meaning, almost like humanity's belief system. An object, word, or idea does not only function in a singular way, but as a conceptual web operating within a set of stipulations.

When we look past the apple, we see how we've constructed all of the world around us:

- Men and women exist in the world.
- Some animals are friends and others are food.
- Correct grammar usage signifies intelligence.
- Trees are pretty but sometimes they are good for homes or paper.
- You must get an education and find a job.
- Education means that you absorb a lot of information over time.
- The more time you spend stationary, absorbing knowledge, the smarter you are.
- You must have a paper stating your time spent absorbing knowledge in order for others to believe that you are smart and worthy.

- Even if you do not fully absorb said knowledge, this paper proves your worth.
- If you read books and do not get a paper to prove it, it doesn't count.
- Only jobs that accentuate intelligence are of true value.
- A proper family consists of a mother and father.
- Same-sex marriages are acceptable now. We guess. As long as you exist within certain man-made borders.
- Mother and father should sign a paper stating their intentions before procreating.
- Wear clothes when you are outside.
- If you don't wear shoes, you are crazy, or worse: poor.
- Say "hello" when you encounter another human. Follow up with "how have you been?" And never truly express your honest emotions within such an interaction.
- Grape poisons are exponentially more luxurious than grain poisons.
- You have failed at life if you have not found another human to forever inhabit the same space as you.
- Give desirable objects to friends when they have occupied a new dwelling.

As we grow accustomed to the world, the rules that have been laid out become accepted, lending more validity to them. When we veer from the "truths" expressed, we will try to normalize our behavior by convincing others of our true nature, or we will hide our behavior from others, afraid that they will reject us, or we will ignore our nature in favor of the accepted norms. We may see this appear in a few facets of our life, but what we fail to see is the entirety of the construction. All of life expressed through human language, behavior, and action is mere interpretation, an accessible yet incomplete depiction.

Language and grammar rules were created for the purpose of establishing a standard for communication. A template for interaction and unity. A coming together. In the advent of technological advances, the increased speed and frequency of communication have shifted written (and typed) word to reflect contemporary speech; diction and syntax emulate feeling, meaning, and personality in new and inventive ways. We can m a n i p u l a t e the structure to suit our motivation and purpose. Insert emoji.

This evolution of language grants us freedom and linguistic exploration, but it still comes with its shortcomings, inevitable misrepresentation. Much can get lost in translation.

We can look at how certain words hold great weight or significance within our cultural landscape. "God," as you might suspect, comes with its own truckload of meaning. A word that was meant to signify the great e x p a n s e and the divine essence of being has mutated into an overworked symbol for an anthropomorphic deity up in the cotton candy clouds. It's lost its zeal. Too much baggage. The same goes for Allah, or Vishnu, or any of the equivalents. Even Oneness, or the Universe, or Source.

For clarification: when using terms like "God," divinity, or essence of being, I simply mean to talk about the underlying energy and connection that encapsulates all living things (and beyond). There is no word in the English language that could capture this (or any other language, for that matter). I could make up a new one, but any other word that I could create would equally fall short. What has saved some of us has segregated others. Words are both powerful and sometimes misleading. The duality continues. You do not need to subscribe to any one religious school of thought in order to get on board with the fact that all is energy, that energy is at the core of existence.

Step 2

Accept that you have been living in a conditioned environment full of conceptual baggage and seemingly objective guidelines to life that are, in fact, just made up.

SO WHY DOES IT MATTER?

Whether we are conscious of it or not, all beings are attempting to return to their essential nature of oneness (that is: of wholeness); it is, after all, our underlying, intrinsic foundation, the energetic connective tissue of existence. When we align ourselves with the interconnected nature of all things, the result is a sense of fluidity and expansion. When we see the world as disjointed and outside of ourselves, the result is separation and isolation. Everything in the physical world is attempting to reconcile the visible reality with the essence of *being*.

How do we know such a thing?

On the most fundamental level, everything is energy. You, me, Ben, and Jerry: we're all made up of energy. All of what we can see, and that which we cannot, intermingles in a divine dance of particle, space, flow, and frequency. Even our thoughts combine and canyengue in this vibrational vortex of b e i n g. There is no escaping it. There is no duck, weave, and go incognito. In every moment, we are making our energetic contribution. All of life is connected in this way, a magic that we have long since forgotten. When we r e m e m b e r and honor the natural state of the universe, of this synchronistic entanglement, a greater sense of ease opens up for us. It is no longer "me," but "us." This is oneness. This is divine f l o w.

Let's start fresh with the individual/person.

The search for wholeness is constant and everlasting (from birth to death). In every moment, day, week, year, lifetime, the person seeks oneness within themselves and, simultaneously, with the whole of humanity/nature/the cosmos. When we are authentically whole, we can connect with the s o u r c e, if you will. Or, in simpler terms, the person will attain true and authentic happiness (not the short-term happiness of a creme brûlée donut, but a deep sense of completion). To be whole is to be attuned to our innermost purpose: to be balanced in mind, body, and spirit. To express our sacred gifts for the betterment of the self and the collective body. A symbiotic pleasure wave. An energetic ice cream social. Love as oneness (sometimes the cheesiest things are the best things, amiright?).

Sidenote: If you're anything like me (or how I used to be, let's say), you release this internal, exhaustive sigh whenever someone mentions hallmark-card-like expressions meant to rattle your meek little heart. "Live, laugh, love" has held the throne as the alliterative punching bag of your ego. The placards. The pillowcases. The coffee mugs! I get it, you know? We get it! The thing is, we might want to have to dismantle the cold-heart castle a little bit if we ever want to get in touch with the true, authentic self. Mantras aside, ya can't mold hardened clay.

But alas:

Some attempts at attaining completion yield lasting results, while others present as clever emulations. Disguises, some might say. This is the distinction between authentic and inauthentic wholeness. It's purely up to the individual to make the distinction. Ah yes, the joys of leading an autonomous life. The challenges that we face merely act as guides for what we need to work out within this lifetime. Where do I need to grow? Where do I have blockages? What triggers me?

Think of every time you attempt to "fill the gap" of boredom in the present moment with an alien meme. And then a Google search about what really lurks within Area 51. Then a follow-up YouTube assignment about Scientology. Then that enchanting video of Tom Cruise bouncing on Oprah's couch, fueled by L. Ron Hubbard's secret sauce. We are endlessly attempting to bridge the gap and return to wholeness, which to us is essentially a sense of satisfaction and ease—an effortlessness, and subsequently (sometimes) a relative unconsciousness. In a concerted effort to become whole, we drift away from ourselves and just so happen to end up in a vortex where cats masquerade as Whoopi Goldberg.

Was the present moment offering you a chance to fill it with something (in)valuable? Or was the present moment inherently complete, in and of itself? That's up to you.

Living life in a way that produces sustained, consistent unity (within the self and the whole) leads to a fulfilling and ultimately pure and happy life. A zesty lil sumfin.

Typically, you can pinpoint inauthentic wholeness by purely looking at it. You can f e e l it. Temporary satisfaction might be a cheat day that slowly creeps into a perpetual treat-yo-self hedonism. The desire to appease your gluttonous self via cheesecake and gallons of rocky road eclipses your long-term fulfillment of avoiding diabetes and arteries with blood flow in slo-mo. Suddenly, your nearsightedness is in top form. Inauthentic wholeness might also take the shape of complacency: wading in the ease of a mindless job for the sake of relative comfort.

When we speak of love, we often think of a conditional love that relies on some sort of reciprocal gift in return. Love as it relates to oneness is so enormous and all-consuming that to limit it to the word "love" is almost to bastardize it. The word "love" is used so frequently and with such misuse that the collective society has a gross misunderstanding of its real and fundamental nature. No other words that exist in the human language come close, so we will have to make do. Words such as "happy" and "love" are so wrapped up in their associated meanings and interpretations (see also: "baggage") that we are sometimes unable to look beyond and fully grasp the power that they hold.

You might think, *Well that's not me. I love my family/spouse/children unconditionally. I know what love is, you crazy garbage person!!!* Well, absolutely! You sure do. Now what about your neighbor? Your enemy? Yourself? Do you love all of these simultaneously? Sorta, kinda?

What if I told you that the only way to truly live in love was to love all beings with unlimited scope and magnitude? How might you unpack that? Hey, don't shoot the messenger. That dude Jesus said it.

That's right, ya gotta love Pigeon-Hoarder Dan, your ornery

neighborhood packrat, too. You know what? Dan has a particular, exclusive stench and that's ok. He's going through something, all right? Dan needs love too, ok?! The pigeons are multiplying at an enormous rate and he needs our help now more than ever. No, but seriously:

To make matters worse, the way we have thus far experienced happiness and love in the context of our everyday lives has led us to believe that their presence is short-lived. The presence of love will eventually lead to some lesser alternative. Happiness can only lead to sadness, and even if you are happy now, attaining lasting happiness for every day of your life is unobtainable and unrealistic. Right? But: love penetrates deeper than the surface level. It's shovel and soft soil. It isn't what we've made of it.

Happiness versus temporary satisfaction.

Love versus lust or I-like-you-kinda-but-only-if-you-like-me-too conditional giving.

Wholeness versus human discount buffet.

People attempt to become whole by an assortment of methods. Consider the search for true love in a romantic partner. Filling holes in our lives is another attempt at rectifying the absence that we p e r c e i v e. In a desperate motivation to "fill up," we turn to friendships, family, lovers, people in general, monetary possessions, drugs, careers, Netflix...Dan has his pigeons...and on and on. There is nothing wrong with striving for things in the physical world, but the perception of emptiness is merely an i l l u s i o n. We were always, and will always be, whole. Our human form, complete with the always-inquisitive mind, casts doubt on this truth, forcing us into a treacherous and never-ending game of hide and seek, when what we're looking for already exists within us. People can add to our happiness, but they cannot be the sole benefactor.

With that being said, there are two ways to go about things:

Understand that wholeness never left us, thereby going forward with that knowledge, and pursuing things for the sake of pleasure and continued unity.

Attempt to find wholeness through various people, things, and events (those of which appear to be outside of us) which will bring forth an endless quest for completion.

All answers dwell within you. Intention is everything.

Next is the collective:

If certain truths exist for the individual, those same truths also exist on a grander scale. Microcosm & macrocosm. All systems and collective bodies—when acting in accordance with divine principles—flourish, nurture, and allow for greater unity. When corrupted, they serve to dismantle, sever, and, well, destroy (morbid, I know). The more people involved, the more opportunity for shared growth, and also, coincidentally, the more opportunity for division and degradation. Our job as human beings (if you see fit) is to recognize when the systems once used for connection and community are no longer serving us in the same beneficial ways. I see you: education system, government, music industry, insurance companies, medical field, etc etc etc.

When things (all things: people, instances, objects, whatever) act in a state of flow, all is serene and connected. Who wouldn't want that? One act in the interest of oneness leads to more of it, while instances of separation lead to more of the same.

Step 3

Acknowledge and honor your inherent wholeness; you are (and always have been) as you should be. Doing so allows you to open the portal of expansion, connecting you more fully and consciously with the energetic field around you.

SEPARATION AND DUALITY

how we process the world

For this, we will need to delve into the human experience and the world of d u a l i t y.

As children, we simply existed in the world. Before contemplating the moral code of humanity, we just lived. Every human in existence has been pure at some point in life, unfettered by our omnipresent cultural conditioning.

We talked earlier about the categorization process that a child learns at an early age (the apple, for instance). Expanded from there, we are given insight into the world of duality: Right/wrong. Good/bad. Winner/loser. Pretty/ugly. Smart/dumb. Dominant/subservient. and so forth. Anything that does not entirely encompass oneness will inevitably be tossed into the lion's den of duality.

Throughout our lifetime, we are subjected to these dualities and experience them for ourselves. Some instances feel bad and others feel good. Since all things in the physical world are working toward oneness, good, by comparison, seems closer to oneness than bad. Nothing, however, that exists in duality can truly encapsulate oneness — by definition, it's impossible.

The first foray out of the state of purity is a complete shock to the system. You are catapulted into the realm of duality, and you don't know what to do with yourself aside from over-correct the subjective "wrong" that took place.

So, something happens and you register it within your new-found understanding of duality.

Let's say something "bad" happens. You do something "wrong"/"bad"/"immoral" and you get punished by your parent. You feel so deeply ashamed and guilty. It's the worst thing you've ever experienced — you're pure, after all — and you never. ever. want to feel that way again. From that point forward, you do everything in your power to correct the mistake, hoping to avert the crisis of the painful wrong. You will always feel right. You will always *be right*. You never want to have to feel that way again! The pain! The agony! Over time, you learn to navigate the world, creating systems and solutions to stay in the safe haven of your man-made protective layer. Obviously, you don't process the interaction with the world in such a way, since you are a baby person and lack the coherence to adequately express this.

The problem is, when you exist in the realm of duality, if you are right, there *has to* be a wrong. Thereby, you create separation, between you and something else. Sure, it feels better than being wrong, but it still misses the mark in terms of achieving wholeness, as long as you attempt to overcorrect in this way.

In this example, you will find every possible opportunity to be right. Your philosophy is right. Your way of life is right. Your attire and your behavior are right. It becomes a mission and it lurks in every corner. Your opinions take over and everyone and everything is at your mercy.

"You're wrong, and you're wrong, and you're wrong!"

"I'm right, I'm right, I'm right!"

Since this classic instance of duality was formed at such an early age, you've been coping in this way for sooooome tiiiiime. As in, you don't even know you're doing it. You think it's in your nature or a vital part of your personality. You know no other way of being. And, hey! It's keeping you afloat, isn't it? You feel right all the time? Good for you, huh?

The thing is, when we are faced with an abrupt and seemingly abrasive instance of duality (i.e., right/wrong), we attempt to overcorrect it because we know somewhere deeeeeep down that our essential nature is being threatened. It's all an illusion, though. Duality can never achieve oneness; it is a pendulum that never ceases.

Example: You are twelve years old. You do moderately well in school despite turmoil at home. One day, your father explains to you, ever so kindly, that you will never amount to anything. Great guy. Naturally, you internalize this. You are a baby person and haven't yet learned that anything cruel dad has to say reflects his own inner disturbances and has nothing to do with you. You get to play scapegoat. Thus, your father — your p r o v i d e r and maker — takes a swift stab at your self-worth, and it doesn't feel so hot. In fact, it's the worst you've ever felt. Attempting to free yourself of this emotional burden, you set out to disprove him by way of academic success, athletic achievement, financial gain, the whole nine. You can't be a *loser* if you always *win*. Sure, some victories felt good, but the initial feeling of worthlessness never truly subsided. Existential dread crept in. Why? Because that core identity of 'loser' was wrangled-in to every instance, every motivation. You dragged that energy around with you like a heavyset ghost on your coattails. If you never dispel the myth of being a nobody, that darkness will consistently fester. You will sprinkle your dominance into all facets of your life: work, friendships, romantic relationships. You will unconsciously take up the torch for good ol' dad. You will seek out situations and people that will appease your sense of superiority versus opportunities for your authentic self to thrive, the self that engages with life as if in ceremony and not a brutish survival of the fittest.

Any behavioral code that we've inadvertently set up for ourselves is doomed to fail. No one can be right 100% of the time. We cannot be good all of the time. We cannot be dominant 100% of the time. We can try it on, and we certainly do, but the moment our stance of rightness/goodness/dominance is threatened, we will stop at nothing to correct it — even at the mercy of those around us. What a treat.

There are clever little ways to describe it:

- I'm just forthcoming and direct.
- I know what I want.
- I'm opinionated and I like that about myself.
- I'm a realist.
- I'm a business person and my aggro-and-kinda-roided-out behavior is 100% necessary and justified.

- I'm destined to be the incarnation of the Hamburglar and no one or thing can ever stop me from wearing his skin and his flat, little hat. Gimme those sweet buns!

Statements like these are our mind's tricky little tactic to make our behavior acceptable. We own it.

Maybe we're right m o s t of the time. Isn't that good for something? Well, no. not really. As long as we are unconsciously adhering to the matter of being right, it's almost like operating in survival mode. There is no opportunity to get in! Mayday, mayday! SOS! Can you hear me?! As soon as we start paying attention, we'll notice that we use every excuse to maintain this rightness. We'll scour the internet for things to correct and opinions to insert. Every time we get in the car, it's us against the world. Every driver is failing to see the road like we do. Cynicism invades everything. We use every moment to judge (*Why is she doing that? If I were him, I wouldn't do that. How could she ever even think about saying that?* Yadda yadda). For years, we have incorporated this modality into our lives so that we no longer even see it as a survival tactic. It merely exists as a part of us. Our entirely subjective view and experience of the world takes over.

Right and wrong is a common theme, but there are others.

Over time, we are addressed with situations that shape us. Think about the most tragic events of your life and the lessons you learned from them. Perhaps you were vulnerable at one point and someone took advantage of you. The boy in 6th grade who broke up with you after two days. The uncle who used his authority for unsavory means. A mother who took to the bottle and abandoned all else. From that point forward, you made a pact with yourself to never be vulnerable again. At what cost? How many people were you truly closing out?

It didn't completely fail us, this plan of ours, but it certainly didn't rectify the wrong. We were never going to let vulnerability be a detriment again. We are strong, powerful, guarded. Every time we were hurt, we added to our shield. A few more nails, a bit more steel. But as much as that shield acted as a mastodon metal-vest, it also neglected to allow anything or anyone past it. Hey, some of that stuff is good too! Thus, we're guarded, but at a cost. We cannot pick and choose when we're accessing our shield, because the shield *is one with us*. It has become a part of us, like a mutant phantom limb.

Maybe you wanted to be the fittest, most attractive person around. Compared yourself with everyone around you. Judged others to seem better by comparison. Found every flaw in others to build yourself up. Maybe you wanted to be the best cook, photographer, comedian, scholar. None of these things are wrong, by the way, but what's the true motivation here? What's the *intention?* Is this constant state of striving from a feeling of lack or one of wholeness?

Now:

If we feel entirely complete, is there even motivation to move forward and achieve anything else, or are we destined for a sedentary life?

The difference in striving for something from a feeling of lack and from a feeling of wholeness is such:

When we are feeling *lack*, we are hoping to add something from the external world to our lives, thereby making ourselves *whole*. However, lack brings about more lack. We always find what we're looking for. Sooner or later, this achievement won't suffice in keeping us whole, and we will have to move on to the next thing. This stops at nothing. Our job, our boyfriend/girlfriend/person, monetary possessions, dream body, and so on. Nothing will fill the hole. The more we identify with it, the more it wreaks havoc on our lives, forevermore. Of course, it's doubtful that we're even identifying this lack as a hole in our lives. If you're thinking to yourself *Well, once I get this o n e thing, I'll be truly happy...* that's a pit imitating innocuous fantasy. Abort mission.

When we approach our goals from wholeness, we are doing them simply for the joy and passion they bring to us. It's not about becoming complete. We are happy n o w, and we would be happy with or without this external thing or circumstance. That doesn't mean that we can't entertain a desire, but it won't add some validity to our lives that we wouldn't have otherwise. Embracing wholeness is the act of bringing to life the voluminous, incredible talents that already exist within us. Allowing inherent truth, creativity, and vitality to thrive in full capacity. Allowing the wholeness within us to bring forth the wholeness in others.

(Step 4 spoiler alert)

Be uncompromisingly *you*.

Side note here: Definitely, make no mistake, no one is telling you that ambition or achievements are bad. Quite the contrary! It's a very distinct differentiation though.

If we are wandering through life, attempting to fill a gaping yet illusive cavity, looking for things, objects, people, circumstances, rosé, and other effervescent yet transient pleasures to jam in there and fill us to the brim, well, that will purely leave us with the same feeling of emptiness! Before we find wholeness internally, nothing in this physical world can do so for us. The funny part about that is, as soon as we see ourselves and the world around us as whole and complete, the more abundance arises before us. Abundance brings forth abundance, and lack brings forth lack. The specific ways that we have been viewing the world over time have, in turn, affected our lives in such a way as to bring forward more of it (like attracts like, as they say), like adorable little leeches who think we're like, real cute and won't let go. They follow us. Indefinitely. So, if we're viewing the world in a negative, cynical light, the world will present itself in such a way that perpetuates that mentality within us. It seems so real, continuous, all-pervasive that, to us, there is no other way to relate to the world. After all, everyone else is seeing things the same way we are, right? We're not crazy, right? RIGHT?! Well, we are. At least a little bit.

We're stuck with our very human vantage point while we're on this giant, floating sphere. With that comes limitation, purely because we only have other humans for reference. It's all guesswork and flawed framework, born of the necessity for survival. The systematic categorization of our lives is m a d e u p: we did this to ourselves. Perception is subjective — a construction — even as an individual or a collective unit. The illusion of separation and the duality that appears before us have been the result of our humanness and of our restricted nature while we've inhabited these bodies. We have held so tightly to a stale sense of existence merely because we've learned to settle. But expansion is within our reach. If we can look past the facade, the plastic playhouse, our self-imposed constraints fall away, and a new outlook emerges.

We've chatted (well, I've chatted) about the moments in our lives that craft us into the human constructions we are. An event, or series of events, unfolds that places us into a negative mode of being, whether that's an amorphous blob-like lethargy, anger suitable for the deepest circles of the inferno, or sadness that seems to pay homage to every Bright Eyes lyric of our emo-stained youth with remarkable consistency. Going forward, we act in such a way that (hopefully) prevents such feelings from arising again, but that plan ends up being faulty because attempting to control the external world around us to suit our individual needs and wants is no easy task. In fact, it's impossible. When we write the script for how things *should be* according to our subjective viewpoint, there are literally countless opportunities for error. You set yourself up for utter, crippling failure.

Let's not only consider the personal narrative here, but the social, national, global, and otherwise.

We are born as individuals in a distinct family structure. It doesn't really matter, for the purpose of this example, what the structure is exactly. Consider the narratives taken by our parents or caregivers, all of their respective beliefs and life experiences that have shaped and emboldened these behaviors and stories: our mom's unrelenting addiction to Freud and bearded men, our dad's sample-platter approach to love, the weekly routine of church and highballs, the school-above-all mentality that melts us from the inside-out.

Now, we are under the care of people who have very specific goals and objectives for our lives. They try to guide us with their wisdom and love (albeit from very skewed and individualized perceptions of the world), but, you know, we're destined for a life somewhat tainted by Freudian beardos. So be it! We may either take these narratives on as our own, or we may discard them. Despite our vision of their actions and way of being, this is the only way that they know how to exist in the world. If there were a better way known to them, they would do that. *No one intentionally suffers.* If someone appears to suffer intentionally, it is because he or she does not see a likely alternative that would offer more joy than their current plan of action.

Think about it: someone spends at least 70% of their day complaining. Do you think that they're doing that to be cute or something? Nahhhh, dawg. In some way, the avalanche of furrowed brow is easing their inner dilemma in some way. It's a coping mechanism. They aren't trying to annoy you for the sake of making a mark on the world.

Your specific lot in life is unique to you. Your parents or caregivers, your nation, your religion (if you have one), your siblings, your year of birth, everything. You see the world through a very specific lens. Sure, people might be seemingly able to see things from your perspective, but not entirely. In actuality, not ever. This might strike you as objectionable initially. You're very particular, you human. You have been living in a specific way for a very long time. You have seen what works and what doesn't. You've examined your mistakes and your advancements, all to work toward a better life. We're all doing it. What we need to also see is that everyone in existence is doing the same damn thing.

Until we've walked, slept, eaten, and dreamt in another's place for the entirety of their life, we could never assert our own opinions into the mix. We simply do not know their struggle.

I mean this for everyone. Not just the drifter down the street who we critique from afar: our mother, our father, our sister, our brother, the ex that we despise, the coworker who sucks, and drives a PT Cruiser on purpose. Everyone has undergone events in life that have collectively added to the patchwork of survival techniques to get through this thing. Most of the time, we don't even know that we're doing it. It's so deeply embedded in our mood, stance, facial expressions, sarcasm, judgment, and victimhood that we literally cannot see through the shit.

Oh, but it's in there. It's in there r e a l good.

You've been judging Samantha haaaaard for her constant need for male attention: the bejeweled acrylic nails, the pouty lips, the intense cleavage. The horror! Maybe Sam has deep-seated abandonment issues stemming from her childhood and she just wants to be seen. or. Maybe you are dealing with some internalized misogyny yourself and feel threatened when other women express their femininity. The judgment of Sam has nothing to do with her and everything to do with you and what you're making her actions mean.

Acts that seem like the most threatening and personal stem from a deep pain that has resonated for a long, long time. It's a buried unconsciousness, a startling act of separation that has reverberated consistently thereafter. When we recognize this about all "abrasive" acts done to us, we finally get to remove ourselves from the equation.

It really has nothing to do with you, and everything to do with how that person has interpreted life.

So now what? We're in the trenches, face-to-face with a deeply unconscious person and we know that nothing they say has anything to do with us. Get comfy. This is not calling us to judge this person. They are merely existing in the world and interpreting form. Existing in the world is not bad. It just *is*. Anything outside of oneness is separation, and the only thing that would solve separation is an act in the interest of oneness (not, by contrast, more separation). Oneness = empathy, seeing the similarities in human experience, and anything that promotes a greater connection.

Therefore, we can shove all judgment to the side. Or try to, right? (Our specific trajectory in life would lead us to certain right/wrong assertions about behavior that are just as individualized as the acts of the person in front of us.) Instead, see this person as an extension of us. No, not resist or cause more conflict by casting ill will upon the person. Only through recognizing our shared humanity can we dissolve our false barriers. The suffering of the other in many ways reflects our own suffering. Only through this channel — that of understanding and acceptance — do we approach reconciliation.

Step 4 (cont.)

Since you know that we're all basically enveloped in a giant, man-made construction, you now have the power to make life up as you wish. Abandon the fabricated ideals imposed onto you by society or your family or whatever else. Sure, it comes with growing pains. Sure, not everyone will totally get it; they're conditioned, like you were, to live life by a set code. Living authentically is *not* merely adopting someone else's dream as your own. You were born into this body with desires, preferences, inclinations, and talents. Nurture them! Explore that shit. Get back to the basics of who y o u are. Be uncompromisingly you.

Step 5

Let others do the same.

NARRATIVES IN COLOR

From the time you enter this planet, you see the world through your own distinctive color palette. For the sake of this exercise, let's say that your visual plane is that of a pale blue tint, maybe something Tiffany's or just-plucked from the laced sleeve of a wedding day bride. This is the starting point. You assume that everyone else views the world with this tinge of lagoon. Why wouldn't they? You have no other source to reference aside from your individualized vantage point, your own two eyes. And clearly everything is a little bit blue. An objective truth backed by surefire evidence.

So, there you are: backstroking through the mellow waters of your cerebral cerulean, until something happens. Gasp. Your father is angry. You are the cause. Your dad, after all, tends to demonstrate his temper, but this time it erupts with a vengeance, almost volcanic as if roused by Mother Nature herself. Every time the anger unfurls, his coloration deepens into a rich fury of maroon. Time and time again, his color slips from light pink, to rose, to Amazon ablaze. His blue tint vanishes without your conscious knowing. It was so gradual! And it's not only your dad: every man, it seems, takes on this reddish glow. Betrayal's heavy aftermath. It's become so commonplace that you scarcely notice anymore.

That's just how it is — the red — and the women around you agree that all of the men exhibit this unsettling tomato tone. We reach the consensus: men are r e d.

It's not only men though. Every little experience you've had has changed the color of your world in minute ways. Ways that are, to you, maybe even undetectable. The slightest little alterations, day by day, over time, have crafted your view into a very colorful, yet very subjective paint-by-number.

You're mauled by a dog, thus, dogs turn grey. Each day, each dog you encounter slinks further into the grey scale, solidifying the memory of your trauma.

America wears white. Japan boasts cream. Christianity in chartreuse. Islam dusted in bronze. Not sure about Hinduism but you heard it's melon.

Money was the source of emotional upheaval in your household growing up, so each time you handled it, the crisp green devolved into an embittered evergreen, and eventually, black. You never wanted to touch the stuff after that. Even those who managed it reflected a sickly yellow color, jaundiced and deranged, biologically askew. *How could they go around like that? Couldn't they look in the mirror and see their monstrous illumination?*

Cars turn orange. Chatty Cathies melt into olive. Women with long hair fade to purple. Alcohol: navy. Schools: lilac. Workplaces: brown.

Depending on your experiences, both desirable and not, your world fills like a Crayola-battered coloring book. The tints change ever so slightly, so even you cannot distinguish between today and the day before, or the one before that. To you, this is how the world looks. In fact, it's so real to you that you assume everyone sees it in the same general scheme. When you think of how it once was — a delicate, soft blue — even that seems like lifetimes ago. *And was it even blue? Or was it more of a cyan? Or are you misremembering? Was it seafoam?*

The reality of your color wheel cannot be dismissed. It enriches your experience during the full evolution of your person. It is the never-ending cinema of your mind's eye. You never really stop to question the color of your world because it's right there, circulating before you without pause. You look for information and events to strengthen your case. You convince others to see the same colors. *Look! It's right there! Why can't you see it?!* For the ones that can't see things as you do, they're dumb or blind. Clearly. You surround yourself with people who *get it.* The smart ones. The ones who know a thing or two. Why waste your time on the others? Maybe they'll wash their eyes out one day and join you on the other side. Should luck strike.

Even if you slap some primer on that bad boy, you still have that chlamydia-pink lurking underneath, or that dungeon-onyx left over from your black magic Wiccan phase, and that Sparx-Yellow No.5 from your screamo high school episode. You can roll on another hue, but the layers remain.

Of course, we're keenly aware of the various viewership modalities. Lenses with differentiating style, opacity, thickness, and prescription haunt every eye on the planet. We know this.

We know that the way in which we see the world is entirely individualized.

The color, shade, and vibrancy of everything in our own world could never be properly articulated to someone, because, quite frankly, *we* don't even really know. After all, you thought that the world was blue in the first place, remember? Sally over here thought it was beige. Billy thought it was peach. To them, that was normal (and every change in shade thereafter). The minuscule variances are lost in translation. Every single one of us sees the world in such different and specific shades of color that it's literally impossible to see things from another's perspective. IMPOSSIBLE. A b s o r b. It is not possible to see someone's point of view in the exact same way that they do. To do so would require time travel and a full investigation of their every waking hour. Objective reality is not accessible to us. Sure, you can try and throw their lens over your own, but then your view of their view is, in essence, your interpretation of their interpretation.

Confronted with the dissenting voices, we steadily morph into the diehard extremists of our own discovered truths. We grow angry, dense with frustration, and listless. We wonder how someone could hold an opinion so counter to ours.

Don't we live on the same planet?

Same country?

Same city?

Same street?

How exactly did we get here?

Remember again that people never intentionally suffer. They're making decisions that will bring them (they think, at least) some semblance of happiness, whether that joy is short-lived or aimed for the long-term. Temporary relief from pain. Whether you like it or not, they're attempting to act in their own best interest. Just as we are attempting to make them wrong according to our own stipulations about how one should live.

Layers upon layers, shadow over shadow.

There is no *perfect* action, place, person, circumstance. Individual people construct subjective conceptions of perfection based on experience and interpretation.

Whenever we catch ourselves wondering why someone isn't seeing things exactly as we are, we know that they are incapable of doing so. Our way isn't *right*, and neither is theirs. *It just is.*

This isn't to say that we should forfeit our slings at the foot of Goliath. Surrender and wallow in a sea of nacho cheese. Hibernate forever and binge every season of *The Office*, again.

The challenge emerges, but we are up for it.

Each day we experience our world, it alters a bit, either strengthening, deepening, or softening the rainbow before us. We've gone about it in this way for as long as we can remember (and even before that). It's been very useful to us at that! We've made out ok, as far as we can see.

But just because our colors have served us well doesn't mean that they suit every eye. Every human deserves the freedom to choose.

After all:

Your blue is their green. My pink is her orange.

Underneath all of that color is a blank, white canvas, and only we have the power to douse it in paint.

Step 6

Identify what umbrella "colors" or perspectives you've superimposed onto your life. Do they serve you well?

Think of any times you've tried to make someone else see the world according to your own color scheme. When have others done this to you?

Let it go. Let it ride.

NARRATIVES EXTENDED

Since birth, you have been constructing a narrative. This narrative is shaped by your family, friends, behaviors, events, talents, community, and environment. Good, bad, crazy, sexy, cool, or otherwise.

When you're young, your specific lens of perception is altered and shaped by the influence of your parents and caregivers. As you grow, the people closest to you (family, friends, and authority figures) continued to help you assimilate in the world and assist you to find your bearings. To no fault of their own, their respective narratives interact with yours in a way that both bolsters their narrative and adds to yours. Think of the parent-child dichotomy and the subsequent energies at play.

Events took place, both positive and negative, which both strengthened your narrative and allowed you to embellish your life with meaning and worth, like a little Christmas tree in your heart with its man-made, and perhaps artistically challenged ornaments.

For the negative events, you learned lessons and rules for the future to protect yourself from further harm.

Like that time Donna decided to spin the wheel on the combined activity of prune juice consumption and hula hooping. A seemingly innocent pastime turned unexpectedly violent and burdened by the trots. (Great take-away lesson though, Don.)

For the positive events, you learned how to go forward with continued success. Like when you discovered that you could Postmate yourself a grip of red velvet cupcakes and eat them from your couch in both glory and deep-seated but palpable and, simultaneously, bearable shame.

For each day of your life, influences have shaped, defined, and emboldened your developing narrative. These influences have been both within your awareness and outside of it. Conscious and subconscious.

Your narrative has been your security, knowing nothing else. It has been your trusty sidekick. Your route to success. Your safety blanket.

You seek out people, places, things, and events that will add depth and assurance to your narrative: a self-fulfilling prophecy. an echo chamber.

As you grow and incorporate yourself into the world, you combine your narrative with others' and, as a result, collective narratives expand.

Your family narrative strengthens (think cultural makeup, socioeconomic status, work mentality, nationality, personality, location, size). Maybe you're a big immigrant family who had to work painstakingly to figure out the grips of a foreign country. Maybe you're from a rich and influential family with a healthy dose of political ties. Polish, Mexican, Italian, or a mix of several. Maybe you're a combo bag with a Neapolitan assortment of loved ones. Whatever it is, your family has a constructed narrative of which you're very much a part.

Outside of the family, a community narrative emerges. Maybe you're in a small town with mom-and-pop shops, cheese curds, and church group sing-a-longs; a lotta white, a little racially insensitive maybe. A little sheltered. Maybe you're in a bustling big city with high energy and a varied patchwork of people and backgrounds. Maybe you've been in one, two, or three cities for a number of years, each with a different story. Whatever the case may be, the community and city has formed a distinct story that has solidified the general assumptions at work. Each individual within the environment helps to shape and define the collective plot. Consciously or not, we participate in this little storyline game.

Within and throughout communities are other narratives. The artist community or the scientists. The collectors. The punks. The homeless. The foodies. The suburban soccer moms. The alcoholics at happy hour. The philosophers. The dreamers. The others.

Each person is a narrative within a narrative within a narrative.

Further out from the community and city is the state. Further out from that, the region. As we scale out, more and more narratives are made apparent. The western part of the

United States has a strong narrative that counters that of the eastern United States. Even so, certain areas within each have their own stories and agendas.

The more people involved, the more solidified and defined the narratives s e e m. And perhaps they are! And yet, they're all made up. Stories only seem real because so many people regurgitate them.

Each country possesses a narrative that's been shaped over time. America: land of the free, with its range of entertainment and people, Santa Monica nose jobs, body posi Instagram models, orange-tinted Leader of the Free World. France: its delicate, winding streets, divine baguettes aplenty, and laid-back sexual culture. The story of India. or Iceland. or Brazil. In each man-made territory, a story emerges and strengthens with each passing day. Leaders are praised and holidays celebrated. Children learn the history of their sacred country, their ancestors, the struggles that empowered the people over time. All of these things allow for the narrative to thrive. The narrative gives people comfort and purpose, a pillow to dream on.

The narratives of the countries interact and influence one another. Think of the wars, the religious strife, and the battles for land; the strong economies and the developing nations; the leaders and the savages (not mutually exclusive). All strengthened by people and people alone. Time, history, and repetition. The larger the narrative, the more vigor and believability it garners.

The richer the narrative becomes, the more opportunity for power, and the equal opportunity for corruption, of suffering on a massive scale. What begins as a coming together of people and minds, easily devolves into a modality of destruction under the guise of unification. Take governmental bodies, which aim to organize and harmonize, but often times get infected with the ill will of avaricious leaders. An honest objective for the whole deviates into an impure goal for the few. This separation bleeds into the masses.

Everything in the physical world is attempting to return to its natural state of oneness, but the threat of separation and suffering is always brewing nearby, waiting to overtake the efforts at any given moment.

When you consider yourself and your specific narrative, you realize all of the other narratives at play in determining your view of the world. Not only have you been crafting your own spin on things, but your family, friends, community, city, country, nationality, ethnicity, religious affiliation, schooling, knowledge base, generation, and time period have all played a very critical role in your development (and the subsequent development of your narrative).

Not only that, but you've been very clever about solidifying the narrative of your life by casting different people as characters in your story. Your mom. Your dad. Your sister and brother. Your best friend. Bob the collector of lawn gnomes. Your teacher and your enemy. All of these people you see through a very specific lens. As years go on, their roles become more pronounced. Their actions and behaviors embolden the characters they play in your mind, and your own character. But you're really only seeing them through your specific frame of mind; that is not the entirety of their being. You are engaging with them in accord with the limitations you've set for them.

If you think your brother is an asshole, and you interact with him as if he is an asshole, you're thereby perpetuating his dickdom. Focusing on the rudimentary aspects of his personality will allow for a hotbed of disenchantment. This isn't to say that behaving nicely will transform him into the brother of the decade, but you choose in every moment how you view and react with your environment. Acceptance is the mothership; she beckons you. Maybe your brother isn't simply a stain on the family, but a human being who has been misunderstood for much of his existence. Maybe his outward expression mirrors the way he feels about himself. Maybe it's not really about you and how you want him to be. Attempting to change our reality to suit our preferences is n o t the business. This also does not mean that you should soak in a tub of toxicity for the rest of your life, but getting out of your head and trying to gain a more in-depth understanding of the situation might lend a little peace.

You were given a name, and a body, and a birthplace.

You can only interact with your mother as your mother. She could never see you as anything but your daughter or son or offspring. Your father could never be your son. Your life, in this body, can only interact with people in various roles. It's all a construction. A story. We all succumb to the familiar trajectory of life and happen to catch people along the way.

In the end, we're all just individual humans telling ourselves stories.

In a sense, it's all a fabricated game.

So. Now what?

You realize that all of these influences have done their part in determining your past, your today, and your future.

All of these narratives started with a singular person. A thought from that individual. That thought and that person combined forces with other people and their thoughts to bring about action. Things. Borders. Rules. Groups and ways of life.

Without the people agreeing on the reality of these things (borders, rules, behaviors, etc.), there is nothing. These narratives are nothing short of a human construction. That is to say, they are entirely concocted. Not real. F a k e. But, seemingly so damn real, am I right?! Mind glowingly real. M i n d g l o w i n g.

Since the day of your birth, you've been incorporated into the world, but only seeing it through layers and layers of man-made veils. From language, to school, to moral codes and the law of a governing body... all of this is purely made up and agreed upon by a certain number of people. People have deemed actions "right" and "wrong."

In some ways, these narratives may have served you well. Your familial narrative may have given you pride and roots. Your personal narrative may have given you a sense of identity and a roadmap to navigate your future. Your country's narrative perhaps gave you a sense of belonging. Or maybe the opposite. Whatever your relationship to these narratives, and all of the other narratives elsewhere, you were granted an individuality. You were both original and part of a whole, contributing to the ever-growing design.

But where have these narratives failed you? Do you feel free, unencumbered, and whole? Do you have everything you've wished for? Do you feel amicably linked with everyone and everything?

If not, why? Why don't you have your dream job? Why aren't you in the relationship you've always wanted? Why are you sad or lonely or hungry for something deeper?

It's all you. You're the one steering this ship.

This gives us complete, unadulterated command of our lives.

Freedom!

When you realize that each individual is doing exactly what you're doing — living life according to a very specific and individualized narrative — you also realize that you should take absolutely nothing personally. Everyone is stuck in their own story.

When you do take things personally and see behaviors and actions as a direct threat to you, know that you are delving deeper into your own narrative.

Each person is attempting to live their individual life in a way that allows for a sense of completion. The story and the attached identity only serve as a faulty substitute to the actual feeling of wholeness because we limit ourselves to labels and a narrow point of view. Those people who haven't felt the power and fulfillment from true wholeness are merely trying their best to feel it in the ways most accessible to them. The moment you see someone as an "other" and not adequately filling the role y o u have set for them, you're doing it too. You're making something into a "should be" rather than accepting it as is.

People are merely attempting to act in their own best interests.

Hey, in other words, we're all tryna get by. Get that bread. Make that money, honey! And all the rest, of course.

I am not a victim. I am not an uninvolved passerby. I am very much a part of every interaction and story taking place.

Whenever a feeling of agitation or a lack of fulfillment takes place, it's due to a story being threatened in some way. Someone acts out of accordance with a narrative. Your food is late or your package didn't arrive when you thought it should. Postmates got the wrong cupcake AGAIN (I told you guys RED VELVET!). The light doesn't turn green when you're willing it to hurry up. Your girlfriend didn't come home when you thought she should. All times when you were wanting things to be different were times when you put your constructed narrative as the cornerstone for the way things s h o u l d be.

Freedom is to see through the individual and collective narratives.

So *n o w* what?

Step 7

Going forward, know that you can create whatever narrative you wish. It's in your own best interest and the interest of others to acknowledge life in terms of its essential nature. Surrender to the flow.

Whenever you are seeing things as separate, you are not only creating more of a divide, but you're strengthening your narrative and causing other people to do the same; in other words, you're choosing your individuality over the collective.

Let's say you went in for a job interview and didn't make the cut. If you're too attached to your personal narrative, you might see yourself as a victim, claiming that you were always the right person for the job, and *Oh, Lord! Life is unfair!* Maybe you dive deeper into existential dread, dousing yourself in mood-enhancing substances. You devote yourself to the fantasy of whatcouldhavebeen and cry yourself a fountain of tears amidst empty Oreo packages. In this first scenario, you're denouncing the reality of the situation in favor of your own, limited perspective. Your story gets the best of you. You may bring that negativity into your future efforts, or you may attempt to achieve more simply out of spite. Either way, separation takes hold (you from reality).

Contrastingly, if you operate from a standpoint of oneness, you realize that someone else more fitting got the job, and it doesn't, in turn, prove that you are some inept loser. *Someone else got the job and that's fine.* For whatever reason, that situation was not meant for you. Going forward with newfound acceptance, you will be o p e n to the opportunities that are r i g h t for you. The "failure" of not getting the job was a pivot point. Change gears, reassess.

To acknowledge and bring forward unity is to foster abundance, creation, and wholeness. Love, in other words. That good, flowery stuff.

If it's your ability to construct your own narrative, why not allow it to be one that not only benefits you, but the ones around you?

We must both operate within the world of narratives (as there is no other world in which we exist) and also, simultaneously, see through the narratives. W i z a r d r y, no? Try that pointed hat on for size.

If all interpretation of the world is done strictly by humans, then what, if anything, does existence mean when humans are taken out of the equation? What does life mean? What does the planet m e a n? What does ice cream mean? Nothing. It's delicious.

Outside of the meaning that humans project onto existence, I guess, well, we don't know. To construct a world and the universe from a purely human standpoint is limiting, but it's all we really know. Again, being human and seeing things as you see them is not wrong, but it leaves an incomplete picture of the environment around us. We fill in the blanks with our own perspective, but that perspective is biased, at best. This viewpoint is subject to the rule of the physical world: duality. It's not wrong, per se. But it's not entirely right either. We only have access to the human lens.

If we can shed a little bit of the certainty surrounding our belief systems (on both individual and group levels) and arrive at the notion that we really, by golly, don't know much of anything at all, existential dread dissolves away and a lightness remains.

Like any human idea, philosophy, or school of thought (human, as they are all human and a product of our very specific mind), the larger the movement, the more susceptible to cracks and corruption. What began as a pure intention and a rational thought pattern expands into an otherworldly beast, still operating under the assumption of goodness. This is the work of the slippery ego on a massive scale. The more egos at play, the more imminent the danger of corrosion. And yet, because so many people are willing participants in the matter, the more believable it is. This is how organized religion on a grand, all-encompassing level gets a pass, but smaller cults with similar general principles don't. No one wants to admit that so many people could be so terribly wrong. The level of conditioning and the number of participants asserting the credibility both play a role in the never-ending saga of mass delusion. Eventually, religious and philosophical ideals morph into caricatures of themselves.

By the way, I'm not suggesting that the core ideas that serve as foundational principles of religion are wrong, but merely that indoctrination can lead to an unassailable structure with problematic features. This happens when we relinquish our logical mind and, instead, wrap all faith and hope into a human-made organization with many egos at the pith. It's not the *belief* that's bad but the abandonment of reason. Humans are inherently flawed. Belief systems are flawed. Priests are flawed. (The long history of sexual abuse in the Roman Catholic Church might provide a clue.)

What if we're wrong about the structure of the universe? Or the idea of sin? Of heaven and hell? What if we've lost our souls? Doesn't ice cream still taste as good?

Just as the individual may only experience, and subsequently understand, his/her/their own life, a similar fate exists for groups of individuals. Due to the specific culmination of events that occurs to the individual, he/she/they will process and define the world according to conditioning, innate abilities/qualities, and the multitude of events, circumstances, and situations made available to the individual and to the individual alone. Meaning: even though a singular incident or a number of such incidents may have happened to another individual, the range, order, and assemblage of incidents could only truly be experienced by one particular individual. We can come close to understanding from another's point of view, but it will never be a flawless account.

On a larger scale, this is also true. An individual can only see the world through their specific lens, and the same is apparent for communities, cultures, nations, and collective bodies of people. Thus: religious war. political mayhem. bombings.

When considering the trajectory of a specific nation and the culture within it, it's clear that, though more variation may be at play considering the number of egos involved, events could really only present themselves in a number of ways. The evolution of a culture is not entirely predictable, but not a complete mystery either, course correction under way.

While I've got you here...

The culture, like the individual, relies on a narrative to propel it forward. Over time, the narrative becomes more pronounced and seemingly more fixed. In the case of the collective body, separate narratives are operating within a larger narrative. Take, for instance, the political environment within the United States. Both major political parties (Republicans and Democrats) have their own agendas and perspectives about how the government should operate. They both have their own narratives with particular personalities, but both still exist within the larger narrative of the United States, which presents its own characteristics and storyline (freedom being the main component). Despite the general framework of freedom, the idea of freedom itself manifests in various ways. What does freedom mean and what does it look like? Both parties see the concept through their respective lenses. Of course, within the parties (and outside of them), a range of opinions weaves through the discourse. Despite the complexity, the two-party system appears to be the only option readily available for the foreseeable future, unless something truly disrupts the narrative and forces it in a different direction. Even in the presence of the Independent party, most people feel obligated to choose a side. At least, the one that best represents them and their ideals, though no one party could completely encapsulate the range of beliefs inherent in each group of individuals. Even if something were to disrupt the narrative, one could argue that the narrative was ready for the change. That is, even the disruption was inevitable. The narrative had evolved and emerged in such a way that welcomed a necessary force of transformation.

Let's say, for instance, the two-party system were to flip and flop back and forth for another 50 years. One party takes power for a term or two, followed by the other party taking equal footing. As the transition of power alternates, the two sides get further and further apart, leaning into their respective tenets with exaggerated force. The polarity heightens over time. Sooner or later, the hyperbolized duality may cause the entire structure to implode. Or not! Who knows, right?

What starts as a great, albeit abstract idea (freedom), takes hold of the individual and then moves outward to encompass the whole. Freedom then turns into a situation of duality: Republican vs Democrat. Right versus wrong. Good versus bad. With both sides accusing the other of having their formidable head in the kiddy sandbox. In actuality, both sides are living in a false reality. The duality is completely fabricated by the collective unit. Time, increased population, and continuous unconscious conditioning have all contributed to the false narrative structure. We all want the same things, but we disagree on how we get there. We can A. come together, or B. split apart. Ya know? Duality.

The government, by the way, is another narrative. So are country borders. State borders. Prison. Government rules. School. Religion. We have chosen to structure our humanity in this way, but other options exist, despite being cleverly hidden from immediate view.

The only thing that makes a narrative "true" is the belief in it. Should everyone decide to quit the game and discard the narrative, no structure would remain. It would be both freedom and chaos (subject to the duality, of course).

So, what other concepts have we invented for ourselves?

- The United States of America: Some dudes wrote something on some paper and called it truth.
- Prison: Based on the agreed-upon rules (see above); if

you behave in a way that is outside of these rules, you go into a building for a portion of your life.

- States: Some dudes made up border lines and called the areas different names.
- Ownership of property: You put your name on paper and called it yours. It's basically renting a piece of the physical world for your lifetime. Once you're gone, it's someone else's.
- Marriage: Two people put their names on a piece of paper and said they would be linked to one another for their lifetimes.
- Citizenship: You happened to be born within a specific country (made up border agreed upon by a group of people).
- Human rights: Granted to people within certain areas of the physical world.
- Beauty: An agreed-upon standard of what you should look like. Alterations may be made to your innate physicality to grant you a certain level of attractiveness.
- Race: Based on the color of skin, a story was constructed about who gets what and how much of it. The more people agreed on this narrative, the more seemingly real it became.
- Money: Some people decided that green pieces of paper were worth something. Stacks on stacks on stacks.
- Language: People collectively agreed that certain sounds would represent different objects in the physical world. A string of sounds and the organization of them stand for not only physical objects and ideas, but the relationship between them. When said in different tones, the meaning alters.
- Cultural norms: What starts as a preference for one or a smaller number of people grows into something agreed

upon by the mass majority. These constructed ideas are conditioned into the public so that they become more and more of a reality over time. The more people accept the "truth," the harder it is to relinquish it. Other modalities of communication between people help to further entrench the narrative into the public consciousness. Think: media, magazines, podcasts, the news, TV shows, music, ads, billboards, social media, movies, food packaging, mall mannequins, commercials, junk mail, robo calls, Barbies, greeting cards.

Narratives are not bad. Well, they can be, but they don't start out that way. As humans, we need a certain amount of structure to get along in life. What would happen if no rules were laid out at all? By nature, human beings imitate one another, making the possibility of true individuality (whatever that is) entirely implausible. The mere fact that you wear clothes is based on some narrative. What's wrong with the human body? Who said wearing clothes is a good thing? Genesis comes to mind.

There is nothing innately bad about being naked, and yet, with the sexualization of the human body (due to the collective narrative) and various storylines created around what certain items of clothing mean, the human body has been subject to the rules of the collective narrative, for better or for worse. Nothing is entirely wrong with clothes either! They shield our fragile, flaky skin from the sun and provide warmth... and make you look real nice sometimes.

Clothes were originally intended to act as a protective layer for the human body, and yet the message of clothes has warped into a thing of class, worth, identity, and power.

You wear a suit and all of a sudden you can make decisions for other people. You're a businessperson now. You wear a sheer, slinky dress and you have a bottom-feeder IQ. None of these things innately mean what we've superimposed onto them with our made-up shithouse nonsense. The overarching subliminal messaging infects our every corner and inch.

These narratives have flooded and soaked into our lives with such calculation and trickery that it's hard to overstate. Everything, every thought, has been manipulated in some way by the narratives of the whole. No thought is truly original, because it has been shaped in some way.

Is that bad? No. It just is. It's a way in which we have to exist. There is no other way. B u t we should be aware of it. Peruse it, and use it to the best of our abilities. Cater to our nature, and still deviate from the norm. Float. Keep our head breathing above those damning waters.

Step 8

Assess what beliefs you've subscribed to based on conditioning. Do you actually believe in the principles or were you told that it's the *right* way to live? Remember that *right* and *wrong* are functions of the human experience and the illusion of duality.

If you could discard some of the limiting beliefs you've taken on as your own, what remains?

Who do you want to be?

What do you want to do?

What do you want your life to look like?

The only person stopping you is, well, y o u.

YOU VERSUS THE OTHER

As humans, we can see our flaws with at least a little clarity. As our awareness grows, we realize that we're all imperfect creatures trying to do the damn thang. It's ok to be a baby dumpster fire once in a while, you know?

Sometimes it shows up in the form of "I should stop ____."

I should stop sleeping in til midday.

I should stop spending all of my money on ironic Backstreet Boys sweatshirts.

I should stop watching horrifying amounts of reality TV as an existential exercise.

I should stop eating my weight in potato chips each day. Not only is it grossly unhealthy, but a huge time dump. Literally, I don't even know how I find the hours in the day.

I should stop judging every person who owns a PT Cruiser.

"Should" signifies that you've identified some behavior as bad and justifiably would like to correct it. The thing is, purely changing the habit won't fix your issue because it's not the underlying factor instigating the whole shebang. Surface-level changes breed surface-level results. You may alter a behavior or two (and good for you! really. shit is hard.), but you'll still be left with this unwavering, nagging feeling in the back of your mind.

Some confusion sets in for a smaller minority of people who have seemingly "corrected" all "wrongs" in their lives and then stop to wonder: *K, now what?* The ego is a slippery thing, my friends (more on that later), but if the people in question are then spending the other portion of their time correcting all of the "flaws" in others, then the problem has yet to be addressed.

True wholeness is seeing yourself as complete and those around you as complete as well. Not one or the other. Denying someone's wholeness is to deny it within yourself. When you recognize that you are a living, breathing, beautiful-yet-flawed individual just like Tyler, or Mary, or Billy-Bob over there, the barrier between "you" and "the other" vanishes. We're all human beings trying to work through our endless complexities.

Only you have labeled your action as bad, wrong, unholy, satan's spadework. Only you have the power to label yourself and your world, so choose w i s e l y. There is nothing inherently good or bad (or bizarre) about consuming three gallons of Thousand Island per day. That's not to say that people won't judge your action to do this, but you know... the world's a coloring book.

When you reach the place of wholeness, most of this stuff

will purely wash away. No, you won't be "perfect" (whatever that is), but you won't find yourself engaged in the same trivial self-imposed dramas as before.

So how do you get there?

Shake off your narrative. At least, the parts of your narrative that do not serve you going forward.

Bringing back the coloring book metaphor once more:

If we have the capability of seeing the world in whatever colors we so choose, why would we choose black every time? Sure, it's slimming. We get it. But apart from that, we must realize that we alone are the only responsible party for whatever palette we choose.

Are there things in this world that many people would classify as "bad" or "wrong?" Sure. Rape, mass genocide, incest, and flavor savers all make the cut. Rather than labeling these things as horrific and the product of evil people, see them for what they are: instances of profound disunion from the collective body. That is, a product of the illusion we face in our physical reality is seeing social elements as disjointed and unrelated. That isn't to say that we should pretend those things are good-to-go and throw a bow on 'em, but adding to the mess with hate actually worsens the problem. When it is all said and done, instances of violence are due to unconscious behavior by the individual *and* the collective body. To be unconscious in action is to have strayed so far from the whole that pleasure can only be sought in the suffering of others (and themselves, by proxy). It's a deep, deep void. No one willingly operates from a mindset of aggression without first subscribing to the notions of duality: me versus them.

To clarify: it's not only the individual's narrative that has played a role in their actions. It's also the collective narrative. We're talking giant, overarching unconsciousness that has seeped into the social setting in ways that we never knew possible. We look to the individual with disdain when it's actually a byproduct of mental, emotional, and spiritual unrest on a global, national, regional, state-wide, city-wide (and so on) scale. Part to the whole.

When I say unconscious what I really mean to say is narcoleptic at the wheel of a semi-truck.

Is the person who commits a school shooting the *sole* threat and cause in that scenario, or is something else looming overhead? Should we also consider how the individual has been failed on a national level? Perhaps systemic potholes are to blame as well, like a lack of affordable healthcare, tied with undiagnosed/untreated mental illness; the widespread stigma of such disorders; and the accessibility and glamorization of firearms. Problems on an individual level always have ties to the collective body. Nothing exists in a vacuum.

Any time we pit ourselves against the "other," we're engaging in this mental combat. When an individual ("the other") acts out in a way that is socially unacceptable, it is reflecting the unconsciousness of the group. The only way to help correct this is to first address the separation within y o u. The group has failed "the other" on some level, and attaching hate to an already dire situation is to drive "the other" further into oblivion.

OR maybe that dude is super woke and the group needs some after-school tutoring.

Let's take serial killers, for instance. Yeah, we're gonna get real taboo here. Stick with me:

When considering the brain functionality of many perpetrators, it's clear that something has gone awry in the wiring, low activity in the orbital cortex. Mechanically, the brains work fine, but many of them do not have the capacity to empathize with other humans. Certain feelings, to them, are completely foreign. They relate to the world in an entirely different way than you or I might. Is it wrong? No. It just is. Pair this with early-onset abuse or trauma and you've got yourself a cautionary tale.

The whole nature versus nurture argument comes to the forefront. Something external, in the environment, has to play a role in the development. The distinct brain chemistry paired with the individual and collective separation (expressed in a range of formats) gives rise to a socially deplorable outcome. Unfortunately, this response to the identified crisis leads to a perpetual narrative in which the serial killers are nothing short of pure evil, and society at large has nothing to do with it. This narrative, as you can imagine, doesn't just begin and end in the here and now. This has been a narrative woven through the ages, gaining strength and validity over time. What we see as a clear-cut division between good and evil is actually a collective unconsciousness that has built itself into the fabric of humanity in a very real, and very clever way. Very sneaky, this one. The slippery ego, super-sized style. The most heinous of acts are opportunities to look at the larger structure.

Being ill-equipped to deal with the outsiders of society, our culture is not capable of understanding these humans and their "unusual" brains. Instead, we look at them and think of how cold and disconnected they are. We point to their inefficiencies and beg that some doctor can fix them with drugs or treatments. In essence, we fail them. We give up. We hate what we cannot understand.

As a byproduct, serial killers (pre-killing) are being failed by society, because we, as a collective unit, only deal with what's easy and digestible. We like pretty, put together, organized.

Those who are mentally handicapped, or autistic, or "lacking" in any sense of their physical appearance, are pushed to the side and ignored. Marginalized. They're misshapen losers. Circus freaks.

And we, as individuals, seeing this injustice, try desperately not to be included in the outlier population. We assimilate and do what's expected. We push the outsiders away, hoping that the disassociation will bring us closer to the chosen ones.

We say things that make us feel as if we're gaining a sense of power.

This power is an illusion. It's a temporary fix. A barrier between us.

"I am better" and "you are less than."

We marry, have children, read bedtime stories, and pray

to our Lord. We hide our fantasies and watch porn behind closed doors. We cower and pretend that everything is seaside cocktails and caviar.

In actuality, we're all outsiders pretending to fit some mold that has been built with vigor and consistency over the years. It's all out of fear. Not wanting to be judged. Not wanting to be *the other*. And then, we fail the outsiders who can't seem to make their way into the circle. In their fear, in their plight as the outsider, they do anything to be noticed. Anything for power.

They connect with their rage. They kill.

By no means am I giving a cool pass to these demented fellas. However, when we look at these rare(ish) incidents, we are failing to look at the bigger picture. What is really driving this? Is this cold murder for the sake of an evil mind, or did society at large have something to do with it?

What support is available for the outsider? How are we working as a unit to prevent these things from happening?

Gun reform? Anyone?

Better mental health care?

Better schooling and education?

How are we pursuing the conversations surrounding mental health? How are we, as a collective entity, treating people with mental health concerns? Are we embracing them or sending them to their respective corners?

Considering the variety and scope of human experience, it's fair to say that some individuals are simply more "awake" than others. Meaning, some people have been exposed to circumstances that have allowed for a greater k n o w i n g within themselves. Again, it's not better or worse, it just is. This is not an opportunity to judge or place yourself on a pedestal. It is, however, a significant moment of reflection. A time for expansion. Those who are deeply entrenched in their own personal narratives will only have a glimmer of hope for awakening if the collective consciousness rises to the occasion (a multitude of singular "awake" beings allowing for the group to sufficiently engage).

You might say, then, that those "awake" beings have a responsibility to maintain clarity in purpose. Any instance in which the narrative takes over and selfish gain and/or victim mentality prevails, an angel loses their airy wings. No but really: each instance of unconsciousness leads to further disconnection, more baked-in narrative, and greater unconsciousness that permeates on an individual and collective level. Thus, if we see that we are awake and others are not, and, thereby, use this as a tool for spiritual domination, we're kind of missing the point.

For me at least, I'll catch myself judging someone else's judgmental behavior, and when the irony of that reflection strikes me, I want to dissolve into a pool of my own tears (50% laughing tears due to my own silly and concretely human misstep; 50% guttural ugly tears from my lameness and distinct lack of awareness).

What's important to note is the ability to infuse any situation, environment, and person with love and acceptance. I don't mean this in a *C'mon guys! Just love one another! We're all friends here!* kind of way. Well, I do, but I don't. Let me explain:

When I say love, I mean embracing oneness. In essence, seeing through the bullshit. Knowing that under all the mess (read: self-inflicted narrative) exists a being who has potential, spirit, and a capacity for greatness. It's the personal and collective unconsciousness that has led to the failure on a singular level (the individual).

Each person has come from a state of purity at one (very early) point in life. They merely e x i s t e d, free from conditioning, free from the absurd regulations of our social environment. This is before the world is thrusted upon them. This purity has existed for all of us, and it's a possibility to discard the harsh factoids inherent in your own narrative in order to revert back to this essence. To do it for yourself is to do it for others.

Open up for it. Let it breathe.

So what happened to the purity anyhow? That's just how life is?

Nothing is wrong with living in the physical plane. Being thirsty (in more ways than one), procuring a job to pay the bills, actually paying your bills, buying tulips for yourself on a Monday, dragging your hungover ass to spin class, making seven pounds of spaghetti and accidentally eating it all in one sitting. This is all a part of the human experience. In ways, all of these activities bind us together. Think of how many people had to come together and work fruitfully to produce the food you eat and the entertainment you consume. Everything in your experience has been touched and formed by countless individuals. To engage in these activities is to be a part of the whole. The distortion comes into play when that essence is lost. Selfishness and greed spread their seeds, and something that was once whole and pure has easily transitioned into separate and unconscious.

Step 9

Nothing exists in a vacuum. As the system influences behavior on an individual level, the inverse is also true: a singular person affects the group. This grants us power.

Even if you lead a somewhat typical life by society's measures, you are still inadvertently cementing the larger structure when you adhere to the norm: tying the knot, wearing makeup, popping out babies, following the law, watching TV, driving a car, brushing your teeth. We can conform or we can carve out something fresh. Either way, we are always contributing.

Decide if you wanna keep with the constant or be a disrupter.

How can you make a shift?

OUR "MAKE IT" STRATEGIES

We have been using strategies to "make it" in the world since we were very young. In the same way that we look at an apple and claim it as such, we look at actions, behaviors, and events and participate with our environment in a way that is very similar to that of identifying fruit. We label, judge, and categorize. We say *this reminds me of the time...* and prepare ourselves for an outcome so that we can properly address it. We've been doing this so long that we don't even recognize that we're doing it. It's second nature. An added layer of protection. Our barrier and false sense of security. Survival mode.

In reality, these things that have given you protection are also shielding you from any true connection. You are inauthentic in this mode. You're operating on autopilot.

We are carefully crafting our identities in ways that are long-lasting and omnipresent in our social circles. No one incident is isolated, which gives great weight to every action.

Consider this: you have a relationship with a friend, and this friend thinks that you're selfish. In the past, you have been a person who looks out for "number one" before much else. Sure, you think, *I'm just a strong individual who needs to take care of myself.* You're chill. That whole oxygen mask thing: gotta put yours on before you can assist. Am I right? So anyway, you've built this relationship with her. Then, one day, you think, *Maybe I should do something nice for my friend. I think I'll take her out to lunch.* You offer and the two of you go but at the end, when you're intending on picking up the bill, your friend protests. This is very unlike you, and she's suspicious. In fact, she's so confused about your behavior that she would rather pay than be indebted to you and whatever crazy shenanigans you have up your sleeve. You would never do such a thing, especially not without being prompted.

So what gives?

Your friend can't even see past your selfishness. You've created this for yourself, by the way. She sees you through a specific lens, a filter. It's not that she doesn't think you have any good bones in your body, but you have acted so consistently in this way that your friend is unable to see you in a different light. She loves you, sure, but there is a wall there.

What about the fact that you're late most of the time?

Talk shit on your friends when they aren't around?

Tell itty bitty white lies?

Keep secrets?

Say you'll be there when you never intended to go?

For the record, these are all things I've done. I'm no angel.

The important thing to recognize is how we're performing in our relationships. If you think that the little inconsistencies that you exhibit are lost on everyone else, you are sorely mistaken, my friend. So very mistaken.

Everyone in our lives is taking an inventory of our actions, mentally shelved or not. We've created reputations for ourselves that have solidified with time, effort, and a pool of experience. Luckily for you, if you are all over the board with how you treat people, the ones that have chosen to be your friend are electing to see your good actions over your mistakes (at least we hope). The more you show up for people, the more they'll want to show up for you (the good ones at the very least).

Step 10

Mentally peruse your relationships.

What identity are you crafting?

How do you show up for others? What image are you projecting for the world to see?

LENSES IN ACTION

We touched earlier upon the notion of the individual lens. You, as an individual, see life through an ongoing, subjective, highly individualized perspective. Not only have you seen life through this singular scope, but you've never had the chance to perceive existence outside of your line of vision. A film that never ceases. A very convincing movie at that. Even if your "film," as it were, seems to parallel another's, no two grand cinematic features are identical.

From birth, you are conditioned to see things in a specific way. So, not only are you seeing life through your own two distinct eyes (lending a singular expression), but your environment is shaping you in its own way, too.

Let's look at an example:

Say you are going to experience events A and B. Having first experienced A, you then experience B. You cannot purely experience B, because you have already experienced A. Meaning, A has, in some form, influenced your experience of B.

If a separate someone were to experience B THEN A, you

could arrive at the conclusion that both the first person (you) and the second person had totally different experiences overall.

For the first person (you), experience A colored the experience of B, and for the second person, experience B colored the experience of A. You cannot unsee this or undo this. It purely exists as such.

Now, following the events A & B, both of you decide to experience a third event, C. Having experienced all events (A, B, and C), could you say that both people are now seeing things equally?

No.

Not only were the initial lenses independent, but the trajectories were different, lending contrasting perspectives along the way.

What you could say, though, is that you and the other person might have a good basis of understanding between one another. You both have separately experienced all events (A, B, and C), and can maybe come to some general conclusions as a result. If a third person has never experienced any of the events, they might have a hard time connecting with the two of you. This third person may have experienced events E, F, and G, which were not better or worse than A, B, and C, but surely different.

When you zoom out further, you'll see that events A-G are also influenced by such things as time, people, location, and countless other factors. Not only do the people change, but events and environments change. No two people can have the exact same journey.

Step 11

Yes, we sport unique lenses, but at our core we share a commonality: we are members of the human race. Let's muster up some compassion, no?

Pay attention to when you assume that another person should see things as you do. Respect various viewpoints. Someone with an opinion counter to yours was dealt a different set of circumstances and events during their time on this planet. L i s t e n instead of preach.

EVERYTHING IS ENERGY

Energy permeates all, and yet, this embedded connection appears fragmented to the human eye. Form masks our integrated, ever-present nature. We cannot exist outside of this field of magnetic e n e r g y.

We are only able to see things that are readily available to us: the chair, the person, the house, the Lambo, the Canadian tuxedo that is surprisingly well-executed. We fail to see the atoms, the infrared light, the sound waves, the empty space, the buzzing synchronicity. And yet, we experience these things and on some level we know they exist. We believe in love and hope, though we cannot see them. We believe in the past and the future, though we may believe in these things as purely constructs. And yet, there are so many things that we cannot see or know as humans. To claim to grasp it all would be a narcissistic error of thought. We are limited in our capacity.

Is it possible, then, that there is something that exists beyond us, something that is both undulating in the distance and generating wildly within our bones, something to which all of the religions are pointing, something to which spirituality and science are inching c l o s e r ?

As we advance as a species, our knowledge is not indicating more distinction between these fields of interest, but a greater clarity and similarity between them. We're all so busy putting our heads down and delving into the minutia that we fail to realize the threads that interweave it all. We *f o r g e t* our *shared light*.

We don't have to embrace the golden-throned God of Christianity, or the blue Shiva of Hinduism; each figure is merely a portal through which something expansive and infinite may be made digestible for the human brain. Everything for us humans must be put into language that we can comprehend.

Maybe there is a whisper of truth there. Maybe, just maybe, all of these schools of thought are intermingling in a way that points to something essential to existence.

The language and rituals are formalities, a way of remembering our true spirit. Intention is everything. Oneness is All.

The physical world presents information to us in a continual, disjointed stream. As individuals, we process this information differently according to our authentic nature and the learned processes we've taken on as our own. When I walk into a room, what I see is different than what you might see. I notice the blues and greens, the pizza box over in the corner that is clearly summoning me. You see the asymmetrical design, the yellows and reds, the mid-mod chair. This subjective view of the world is obvious and accessible from our own vantage point, but it isn't (and could never be) an objective view of reality. As such, we cannot (and should not) trust our own eyes and ears to make absolute claims about existence. We can share what is right for us, but have no business claiming the same for someone else, who has lived a very different life than our own.

To know anything for certain is to be misguided.

Step 12

Question, and then question more.

Maybe you consider that this might be a possibility and you then choose to stay in the middle, not wanting to pick a side. Look, I get it. Seems a little egotistical to "know" one way or another, doesn't it? The same passion that religious zealots possess on the one polarized end is mirrored by the steadfast righteousness of the atheists on the other end of the spectrum. How could you know for certain?

The only thing we're able to do is test how different principles operate within our world and use them for our betterment and for the welfare of other human beings.

Even removing morality out of the mix for a second, let's consider this:

You have two options. Both options seem to better your life in some way. You have to determine which choice is best:

1. You go to the ice cream shop and take the last 200 ice cream cones home and store them in your freezer (your fridge is extraordinarily large, for the sake of the example). You and you alone must eat all the ice cream within the next three days. You've got your rocky road and your cookie dough. They even give you some artisanal delights,

such as honey paired with kaffir lime leaf. It's your dream come true. You fuck wit it.

2. You go to the ice cream shop and you are given the 200 ice creams, but you can only have half a cone. The rest are to be distributed to the other 199 people behind you. You're, like, kinda pissed cuz you really wanted at least three cones. You will not be satiated with this paltry share, but you'll survive. Somehow.

So, which do you choose?

Option 2.

Sure, eating a million pounds of ice cream is good for the figure, but sharing the wealth is your best bet. And yes, it's nice to give creamy delights to unfortunate others. Here's the thing: selfish acts in which you are the only receiver of anything really won't help YOU in the long run. Forget the others for a moment. Both acts have short-term and long-term results. What we're aiming for is complete wholeness, which spans the longest amount of time. The gift that keeps on giving.

This is where we are pushing morality aside and seeing things from a slightly more removed approach.

- Option 1: You get to eat a lot of ice cream (swim in it, even), but all of these other people despise you as a consequence. Should you need something from someone in the future, you're damn right that those people are going to remember you as the sweet treat hoarder who devoured all of their hopes and milky dreams. Seriously, who eats that many scoops in one go? We have feelings to consume, brah. At the very least, a flashback might bubble up, which may or may not sway their decision to help you in whatever sticky mess you've got going on.

- Option 2: Sure, you're a little light on your personal dose of dessert, but all of these people will likely remember your kind act for years, nay centuries, to follow. In this one act, you've won favor with potentially 199 people (and their friends, quite possibly). If you needed something from one of them at a later date, chances are a little better here. Plus, you didn't gain a twenty-pound frozen food baby.

This isn't to say that we should do things for other people because we want to fulfill a selfish agenda, but the most powerful deeds are those that ultimately bring the most people closer to oneness. A conscious recognition of you plus the other. Acts that capitalize on our essential nature will reap the most rewards (perhaps not always short-term, but long-term).

Cheap thrills = short-term gain and a temporary sense of "wholeness."

Well-intentioned efforts based in wholeness for you and the other = lasting fulfillment.

We're sort of stumbling into utilitarian ethical territory here, though I don't suggest that any singular universal law can be righteously heralded. Every individual must choose for themselves.

This isn't always so cut-and-dry or painfully obvious. It isn't a sacrifice of pleasure or a denouncing of all worldly desires.

We're talking more in the orbit of *authentic action*. A deep understanding of s e l f and what you have to offer. Only you know this. Only you know how to best honor your body, mind, and spirit.

For me, this may mean a few things: nourishing my body with enjoyable exercise, meditating, reading a book in my bath with a glass of wine, traveling to a foreign land, or journaling. It could mean strengthening social bonds by going out with friends or emboldening the relationship with myself by being dead to the world for an evening. Maybe it's simply forgiving myself. Forgiving another. Sometimes it means skipping the donut. Sometimes it means demolishing that thing *and* his little friends. It often means working towards a personal ambition, like this book. It means thinking outside of the box and sharing my truth. For me, it's about balance, delving deeply into our philosophical underpinnings, seeking adventure, expanding the mind. And it could mean something entirely different tomorrow.

Step 13

What makes you feel complete? Consider the times when you are wholly in flow with the universe, entirely engaged in an activity or interest. It's almost as if your core spirit melts into the larger energetic realm of existence. Thoughts fall away and you simply surrender.

Think of how you might incorporate more of this into your daily routine. How can you feel more a l i v e each day? Each moment?

"PROOF" AND THE EXISTENCE OF A HIGHER BEING

The argument is usually *I'll believe it when I see it* when it comes to establishing the verity for a grand, ethereal energy or presence. Mainly, we'll put our belief structures to bed when we have cold, hard facts regarding the actuality of a spirit or essence existing beyond the physical world.

Sometimes we humans forget about our imperfect nature. Delightfully prone to error. Lest we forget the invention of Cheez Whiz and the metamorphosis of Tide Pods from cleaning instrument to snack. (Cheez Whiz, admittedly, rides the rail between brilliance and sacrilege.) Or the Pokémon GO gamer who ventured off a cliff in search of Bulbasaur. Maybe the human mind does not reign supreme in ascertaining the total scope of the universe? Then again, maybe we have some slight idea of it, a Costco sample-size portion of it. Whatever we know, there will never be essential "proof" in the way we want it, because we are only exposed to that which exists in the physical dimension, and under the strict stipulation of being h u m a n. We do not know all of the answers, and we could never be certain that we've obtained them.

Cultures from every age and geographical location have been clued-in to the spiritual nature of what lies beyond (and within our very core) but it's impossible to capture in its entirety. We're given clever tools, flowery literature, and dogmatic practices, but an all-encompassing "truth" and/or "proof" is impossible here on earth as we flail around in our body suits. It's a gut thing. A thing levitating above our very human senses.

If we haven't understood the inner workings of all that lives and breathes within our present world, how can we draw larger, absolute conclusions about what exists beyond ourselves and our universe? We know nothing and yet we know *something*.

It's a feeling. A mood. When you allow yourself to open, to experience something more than what appears in your fight or flight mode, the world similarly opens up for you. The magnitude that dwells within you aligns with the omnipresent totality.

MORE ON G O D (OR WHOMEVER) AND OUR LANGUAGE BARRIERS

Our vital, energetic basis is evident in all areas of human life, and life beyond the human experience. The idea of wholeness, of universal energy, and of what people call the d i v i n e or God, is both within everything and outside of everything. Science and spirituality are now, more than ever before, joining together in parallel and interconnected ways. For the first time, science is relating to spirituality in a way that emboldens it. Strengthens it. They are not diametrically opposed forces, but two ways of expressing the all-encompassing nature of existence, the essence of being. My man Einstein called it. As a well-known science-god himself, even he saw the great beauty, depth, and mystery of the universe. He denied the existence of a personal God concerned with our petty grievances, but argued in favor of a spirit ingrained within the laws of nature. Cosmic religiosity. Get a dude who can do both. Right, ladies? Right, men? Right, non-binary babes?

Just as the individual can only see the physical world through its own two eyes, the collective body can only see this force of divinity through its limited capacity. For some cultures and communities, this essence is God. For others, it's Allah. Buddha. Vishnu. Energy. The Universe. The range of supernatural beings that have manifested in the cultures in existence now and before our time. They only could express themselves in these ways, which is why our Gods are so different and yet so similar. It's the same divine force at play! How magical, right? How m i n d g l o w i n g. To deny a God in another culture is to deny it in ourselves.

But it's not simply God. We're seeing the evidence of a grand force, an essential and foundational order, an energy that is within and beyond all of us, through a multitude of means. You don't have to be a believer in some anthropomorphic entity in order to see it. It's in mathematics, biology, physics, astronomy, nature... it's everywhere. To yield and surrender to its magnitude and order is to embrace abundance and return back to the source, whatever that means for you. You can still be a nihilist and get up on that flavor. Energy exists within, without, and beyond the scope of our imagination. We literally only know about 4% of the universe. That's the scoop and we're liking the possibilities.

The idea of God, or the revealing of some element of the divine, showcases itself in different ways, according to experience. It's all the same energy but manifested in different formats, figures, and phenomena. This is why the idea of God has shape-shifted according to location, time, group. No o n e idea of God is more correct than another. They are all correct, and yet all slightly wrong as well. To exist in the physical world and subject to narrative is to be cast into an illusion that misses the mark in a fundamental way. A false narrative.

Our language has brought us to a point of understanding, and yet it has failed us. Systems that we've uncovered and built have allowed us to understand and make sense of the physical world, but also be a slave to it. Our relationship with words started at a very early age. We were conditioned to believe in the binding, reciprocal relationship between word and object or idea. "Apple" meant red, round fruit. "Mom" meant the woman who birthed you. "Family" and "friend" meant something very specific to you. At the core, all of these things are energy, vibrating on different frequencies.

As you grew, your relationship to words and objects/ideas expanded and became more permanent. Your world, a world fixated on categorization and labels, placed you at the center of your narration, with the rest of the world to determine in relation to your physical body.

Family, schooling, friends, media, and a range of outlets conspired to showcase a world that was both digestible and agreed upon.

God was presented to you in a few different formats. Your experience with this God and the various programs of belief either allowed you to cherish this figure, resent it, or grow apathetic. From then on, your relationship with the word "God" was complicated and fell victim to the deeply entrenched and long-standing narrative.

You could seek happiness in this God, or perhaps experiment with another God. Maybe Allah, or Vishnu, or yoga, or the Universe. All terms and their associated figures (or non-figures) came with baggage. Baggage of all the people who speak about it and label it.

If a grand, all-encompassing power exists both within and through all of life, could it really be restricted to a single word or human identification? Even if you don't believe, how could you be so sure? We, as humans, know so very little. So. Let's take a knee for our total and complete lack of full knowledge. Let's be a little humble here.

The more words, scripture, rituals, and prayer that are fastened to the idea of God, the further away we get. What starts off as a pure intention — the hope to stay immersed in the love and power of a greater source — derails into an unhealthy obsession with form. Instead of surrendering and allowing for this force to be a presence in all things, we focus on the words, scripture, and practices. We think that these practices and words are synonymous with God, a welcome substitute. Nothing in the physical word can entirely capture the magnitude of the great beyond, the interworking and divine order of all that is. Each element possesses it, but no element can serve as the *only*, supreme evidence.

So, what do we use as an appropriate word for "God" if the word itself, in all of its baggage, no longer serves us? "Ice Cream"? Something holy is going on with that stuff. I'd be down to create some ritualistic exuberance around my pal Cherry Garcia.

In recent years, the newer and evolved schools of belief have transitioned into a use of the term "Universe," which is basically the same as God but with less baggage (for now).

Even with its relatively new emergence, an attempt to stray from the stale beliefs associated with God, the Universe has already taken shape, which will inevitably shift (and already has) into yet another school of thought within the world play. Those non-believers will have the same dissenting thoughts about the Universe as those who now believe in the Universe thought about the term God. It's a cycle that persists. Nothing in the physical world is free from it. The duality will always maintain, outside of oneness. To label it is to distort it. The Universe is now one and the same with other popular modalities of belief and their respective practices. Think: New Age, yoga, crystals, meditation. This is another way that the essence of existence has manifested. In this time. For this population.

Even if we pick a different term, let's call it "Icecreama," keeper of hearts and salivary glands, our Lord and savior... the same rules apply. It will inevitably lose its vigor and fall further from the truth of what it is. Nothing, no word, can truly encapsulate it. To do so is an effort in vain. (And yet, we have to call it something, so...)

Try this on:

Your earliest memory is of your third birthday, when you were delightfully innocent and robed in the naiveté of youth. You remember your mother singing to you, joining in with the chorus of familiar voices, as she brought out your circus-themed cake, a medley of frosted balloons and dancing clowns, with tiny flames swaying on top. The establishment of bliss.

Your first bite is surprisingly cold but satisfying, nothing you've ever tasted in your long, three years. *It's vanilla ice cream!* your dad exclaims. The opiate of the masses, some sort of baked good and frozen delicacy fusion-sorcery. Especially compared to all of the baby sludge applesauce of your earlier years, this shit is killing the game. *Why don't we eat this all the time?* you think. Thankfully, you get to delight in its otherworldly flavor on Sundays and holidays, at the very least.

It's not only the taste that appeals to you. It's the comfort and familiarity. It's the consistency. The coming together of family. The safety and history it represents for you. It's not just ice cream but an amalgamation of meaning. And it makes you feel real nice when you eat it.

Over time, you use ice cream as a crutch. When you celebrate, it's with a healthy pint of 'nilla. When you're sad, you lather it on. It's your tried-and-true. Your ride-or-die.

Somehow, you encounter people who don't quite grasp your cream dream fanaticism. *But have you tried chocolate?* some ask. Sure, you've heard about it, you've dabbled, but nothing compares to your vanillawakening. *What about neapolitan?* others inquire. *Those don't even go together!* you think. *Where did these nut jobs come from, anyway?* Vanilla is clearly fine on its own. No need for the superfluous sacrilege.

After years of overconsumption, your experience of vanilla dulls and it doesn't offer the same emotional support that it once did. You keep trying to r e m e m b e r how it used to satisfy your cravings, but ice cream was always merely the portal, the passageway through which joy and pleasure could be felt. It simply *points to* something larger, grander. It wasn't the *only way*, but *a way*. That same joy could be accessed by way of nature, the stillness of a moment, and music. Every direction and every breath. Contentment and peace are not done *to you,* but arise *within you.*

Step 14

Identify your *G O D.* Where does it dwell?

A WORD ON PERCEPTION

It's easy to cast off all belief systems and claim to your non-conformist friends and dusty leather notebook that they are merely the opiate of the masses. Most of us probably wander in the field of healthy skepticism. In a way, they are: they provide a glimpse into the magnitude of the universe. Some people believe that religion only exists because people can't deal with the fact that the physical world is all there is. We die and morph slowly back into dust. Religion merely sprouted as a coping mechanism.

We crazy humans get to construct some meaning around this existence. Is your world plagued with madness or shrouded in delicate hues? The interconnection between all living things isn't something exclusive to a belief in a higher power. We see this in physics, nature, biology, architecture, sacred geometry, and, simply, all systems that bind us on the physical plane. They all converge and yet parallel and mirror one another in a synchronistic symphony. Everything within these modalities expresses the truth in their own respective languages. You, as an individual, get to pick how you see it, whether that's in nature, or sports, or your romantic relationships. Love and connection are all around us. You don't have to be a believer to get a scoop of the good stuff.

If you're inexplicably drawn to biology (bless you, child), explore that! The deeper you delve, the more you'll tune in to the wondrous and synergistic nature of all living things. Maybe you're John Nash's present-day protégé, a mathematician magician in your own right. Nurturing your talents in this field will reveal the arrangement and formulas that exist within all things we see and touch, without fail. Even things unseen by the human eye. What glorious bliss, right?

Whatever your drive, you have an access point to the rich complexities of the universe that direct us to something much larger than ourselves. Everything is laced together and interwoven in synergistic majesty. Everything is religion.

Do you choose to s e e it?

Lest we forget: how we view the world is, in part, determined by our environment and how we're groomed to perceive the physical world. Western-bred people, constantly reminded of their individuality and independence, might see a room differently than their Eastern-raised counterparts, who are immersed in a culture of codependency and the interrelated nature of all things. The Westerner might focus on a singular object in a room, while the Easterner might see the room in its entirety.

How I fill in the blanks is entirely different than how you fill them in. We are seeing reality through a very skewed perspective. We, as individuals, see the world through a lens that has been affected by the innumerable influences of our lives. These influences are known to us, and some, not so much. We are not aware of how much we've been affected. What we t h i n k we know is a whisper in an all-consuming cacophony. If we're always already seeing the world in a flawed (err contorted) way, why not choose the view that will most benefit us and those in our company? Why not chip away at our own unconscious biases?

Step 15

If our lives might bear even more abundance if we choose to operate under the principle of oneness, why not try it on for size? Slip it over. Choose another route that may be just as skewed, but in a way that serves us as individuals, and the collective.

WE ARE A L L INTERCONNECTED:

THE SYSTEMS THAT B I N D US
& the spectrum that exists in all things

In nature, all of life is intertwined. No matter how disconnected one habitat or organism seems from another, they are all mutualistic, reliant upon one another for survival. One cannot exist without the others. We, as humans, need food to survive, which calls upon the plants and animals to sustain us. Plants need the sun. Animals need other animals and plants to feed upon. Bees need flowers. We all need bees. Queen bee needs her hive. We all need B e y o n c e. Our survival and the survival of all systems within the natural world rests upon coexistence and reciprocity.

At the core of mathematics exists a complex framework that makes sense of our physical plane and beyond. Per Fritjof Capra and systemic thinking, we can understand our physical, corporeal world in terms of a network of interlocked relationships. Every component of life, down to the cell, is a system. To tap into this formula is to reveal the beautiful arrangement of all that we see. Our understanding of the physical world is dependent upon this complex organization. This is precisely why science and spirituality are not mutually exclusive. The more we utilize science and mathematics, the closer we get to our collective spiritual awakening.

At this stage in the evolution of our species, we are starting to truly grasp the interconnectedness of all systems. Like a living organism, each limb, organ, tissue, and cell serves an essential purpose. What exists in the part, exists in the whole. Nothing exists strictly in its singularity. To see disease in one component is to reveal a larger and more integrated issue. All of life partakes in this relationship.

All of life is attempting to return back to its essential nature of oneness/wholeness and the more we embrace this unity, the more successful and fulfilled we will be. Things thrive when in alignment.

What do I mean when I say that all of life is attempting to return back to its essential nature of oneness?

1. An object, being, or part of life is "born" (we will refer to this object/thing as a "being").
2. Before being "born" as a specific object/thing/person/plant/animal, it existed within and a part of the oneness (for something cannot be simply born from nothing; energy can neither be created nor destroyed a la the first law of thermodynamics). For a human, the being was one with its mother in the womb, and even before this, it was one with nature/the beyond/the expanse. Upon birth, the being is only *seeming* to be separate from the whole (as it occupies a particular container/vessel that is its form, in this life). Though, even within this vessel, the being

is still wholly complete and existing within the oneness. Any apparent dissociation is purely a consequence of human thought and perception. An illusion.

3. Consciously or unconsciously, the being attempts to regain its wholeness, fulfilling its life objective. It grows into its body. It thrives and flourishes. It yearns and seeks. Just as the flowers emerge toward their God, the sun, and blossom in full. Or the animals mate, becoming one, and reproduce. The breath of life expands. The individual life emulates the totality.

4. All beings will eventually return back to their essential nature, through the instance of death, which is really a rebirth, or a returning back to complete oneness, everlasting consciousness. Until the cycle repeats again.

Living and dying are the only constants that exist. These cycles perpetuate the underlining theme of completion, which constantly exchanges life for death and death for life. The duality. It's all an illusion. The death of one transforms into the birth of another. Our bodies perish, sending precious minerals and nutrients into the soil, which is then available for the emergence of new life. No energy can be exported without an equal amount of energy infused.

An unconscious life breeds the mental restriction of duality. The next stage of evolution is calling for us to look beyond the polarity. The more of the expanse we nurture, the closer we get to our essential nature.

We can see the beginning of this surfacing within some social spheres. Instead of only female and male, we are witnessing the acceptance of other classifications, such as transgender, gender fluid, androgynous, non-binary, bigender, and many others. Though the act of categorization presents its own flaws, this is a step in the right direction (especially since our historical processes of understanding the world have come through systematic categorization). Like all things, gender exists on a spectrum, just as we see women who possess more testosterone than others, some men reveal more "feminine" qualities than their peers. The stereotypical representations of men and women are so far from how our humanity can be fully expressed, but the distinctions were necessary steps in our evolution. Now, we're asked to step forward and feel uncomfortable. Leap into unchartered waters. Dare to see gender, or sexuality, or identity outside of limiting labels.

The overarching ideologies surrounding gender have permeated every crevice of our culture, further cementing some false reality about humanity that doesn't really hold any lasting, meaningful value.

Our preferences, demeanor, interests, and layers of qualities should be celebrated and elevated in ways that allow us to contribute positively to society and show up for ourselves, regardless of whether or not they fit into our readily available boxes.

What we shouldn't do is attempt to assimilate into the greater whole by strictly representing aspects of the gender we were assigned to at birth. Such tropes are tired and yawn-worthy: pink, floral, long hair, dainty, reserved, football-lovin', emotionally-removed, tough, logical. Sexy-nurse-Halloween kind of predictability. If you're into it, hell yeah, do it, but not for the sake of conformity.

In every person exists a spectrum of attributes, and some of these particulars of self will naturally fall into the half-baked conceptions of what it means to be "female" or "male." Working toward wholeness requires a continuous undoing of these notions in favor of a well-rounded and balanced human being. Our ambitious call-to-action regarding standard gender association and perpetuation must be shed from the collective body. Gone are the days of the straight-cis norm.

Our systemic flaws are showing. Real bad.

We are conditioned to showcase the parts of ourselves that sync well with the masses and shun the parts that don't exactly jibe. In doing so, many of us are repressed, but this unnatural containment of energy will absolutely affect the other areas of our experience, most likely in unsavory ways. What are we missing out on globally as a consequence of this systemic oppression?

The part reflects the whole.

As each individual seeks their inherent truth, calling forth the shadowed energies of our own villainous underworld, so too can the cumulative body.

An acceptance of diversity gives way to a more inclusive society. Freedom of love and expression should be attainable by all people, but we can only look to ourselves first. Where am I blocked? Where must I heal? How might I be ignorant? Light does not exist without darkness. It's in there some-where. I promise. When we start to notice the spectrum that is inherent in all systems, and within our very bones, we can begin to unlock our minds, and maybe even our hearts too.

Step 16

Have you restricted your identity to a label or a list of such?

How can you unleash your innate spectrum and allow it to flourish?

Think of any behaviors or actions you have avoided purely due to accepted norms.

Do them anyway.

Remember that any killjoys are merely products of lifelong conditioning.

They don't know any better, but you do.

INTERCONNECTEDNESS AND A HEALTHY SOCIETY

For a healthy society to prosper, we may point the magnifying glass at the self to determine how our gifts and talents can better the world around us. Diversity is e s s e n t i a l. People who make rules are necessary, and people who fittingly expose the dangers and pitfalls of the rules are useful for the evolution of the collective. We categorize in order to better understand our world, and then those same categorizations can limit us and keep us within their shackles. The more physical, mental, and metaphorical borders we draw, the more discord will exist between all of us, leading to greater pain, a greater *lack of love*.

When we work in accordance with our essential nature of interconnectedness, limitations are eliminated and expansiveness manifests. The only way to unlock the cuffs is to address our bounded limbs, our self-imposed restrictions. We start with the self and move outwards. How are we impacting our world around us? How is our internal garden of flora and fauna manifesting outwardly?

Doing what is right and good for the self, in conjunction

with what is right and just for the whole, is the only way to true, lasting success. Yes, you may do well in your financial and career advancements through only thinking of the self, but doing so will lead to increased separation and pain throughout the whole, and, eventually, to the self. This cannot be avoided. To live authentically and with boundless love, actions cannot be purely for you and your chosen few. Sooner or later, destruction will take hold.

There are well-informed pathways with prescribed avenues for reaching your goals. By all means, use this information to your benefit. The trick is to note that you don't have to meander down the same roads. It's up to you. Innovation is only achieved through the act of thinking beyond. See the routes before you. Pick-and-choose what does and does not work for you.

Let's say you want to be a surgeon. Clearly, there is a very well-defined plan of action for achieving this goal. You could opt to operate on Craigslist surfers in your grandma's basement without the backing of a medical institution. Sure, that's one way of doing it. Or, you know, you could attend school and get the necessary licenses. Abide by the rules of society, and then (if you choose), attempt to see how your skills can be applied or amplified in a new and innovative way. Maybe that means starting your own practice in another country or delving into a different area of specialty. Maybe it means doing really well within your field because that's your objective. Stay in the lines, and then choose to challenge them. Obey the rules and then break them.

Step 17

Ask yourself two questions:

- What means the most to me?
- How am I nurturing that desire?

LARGER SYSTEMS AT PLAY

& how to navigate the constructed world

A singular dependency on any system of thought/belief/ practice holds the potential to restrict the flow of expansion.

Take the medical field.

Western medicine has advanced over the years through the use of technology, and it has served us well over here, but it falls short in diagnosing or treating every illness. Instead of looking at the body as a whole to prevent illness, it is structured in a different way, combating a single problem as it arises. Meanwhile, Eastern medicine considers the body as a whole and tends to approach illness through a more holistic regimen. It doesn't rely on the heavy use of concentrated medicine or opioids, but on herbs, tinctures, specific diets, etc.; despite its integrated methodology, Eastern medicine does not always possess or rely upon the same advancements in technology as its Western counterpart.

In an ideal world, both Eastern and Western medicine would combine forces to provide a well-rounded and suitable approach for any patient, but the obsession with choosing a "superior" schema keeps these systems separate and flawed, a product of the physical world's inherent duality. We approach a harmonious u n i o n with the partnership of multiple traditions. The more inclusion, the c l o s e r we get. That doesn't mean haphazardly adding all aspects of a body of work, but, rather, threading together a quilt of the highest quality fabrics. Seems intuitive, yeah? The simplest answer is usually the best one. Occam's Razor in true form!

The medical field at once allows the human body to attain its health and wholeness, and deviates into a dangerous sector fueled by money and power (even if that means power of the ego). The more egos in the mix, the greater the chance for breakdown.

When we merely go along with the prevailing system without necessary inquisition, we allow it to show up and intermingle in our lives in (sometimes) dissatisfactory ways. When we give boundless power to its representatives (doctors), we cheat ourselves and others out of our potential. Instead, we can question, recalibrate, and move forward with the intention of benefitting the majority.

You may not only consider the pertinent system (medical field, for this example), but the environment and the subsequent narrative elements stemming from it. In America, Western medicine operates within the capitalist arena, meaning that success is often measured by the accumulation of wealth. As such, the medical field and the associated partnerships (drug and insurance companies) have great power collectively, but increased likelihood of maleficent ends. The capitalist agenda infiltrates all aspects of the society like a penetrating, slow bleed, even within sectors geared toward "pure" objectives like health and wellness.

Capitalism isn't *bad* per se (as the opportunity for freedom in economic exchange is valuable) but like any other element within the physical world, its initial intention may warp with time. The more expansive the reach, the more ability it has to destruct.

Grasping this on a macro level and releasing yourself fundamentally from it on an individual level, is key in gaining back your autonomy. You can operate within the system and not be a slave to it. This doesn't entirely liberate you from its clutches, but these systems (though flawed) need to exist for the essential operation of a society. If it wasn't one specific system, another would be at work. Navigating them in a way that serves you and the people around you without merely surrendering is vital.

So what does this look like exactly?

Keeping your head above water.

At every junction, you will be faced with an obstacle. How do you use your environment for not only yourself, but for others?

The interconnection of all things is the only truth we know. It underlines everything, revealing itself in a range of forms; so much so that science and spirituality are expressing their similarities today in ways that haven't been so easily accessible before. All systems express this aggregate in their respective languages: music emulates the feeling and sound of the infinite; mathematics pairs symbol and equation with the complex innerworkings of the universe; culinary mastery allows food to become one with us, granting life, and communion, and ambrosian beauty. It's in everything. We are all exposed to this truth in various ways, but it's up to us to find what resonates and explore within and beyond it, without the superfluous constructs that the larger societal world has put before us. In doing so, we will be one with our nature.

Prescribed ways of being in the world are useful for structure and relative comfort, but other routes exist, and many have yet to be discovered. What good is following a trodden path if it leaves you feeling l i f e l e s s or complacent? Are you living a life that you've intentionally chosen, or have you succumbed to the prosaic timeline of a status-quo life? You are the only one with the answers. You are the only one who can change it or keep it in the same, circuitous course.

You want to write a book but no one wants to publish you? Publish yourself. Or choose a different medium! Old ways can be tried-and-true for some folks, but new ways are adventurous and call forth the true pioneers. If you don't succeed the first time, try again, or opt for another pathway that might serve you better.

Stuck in a job that you hate and you're passing 40? So, find a new job. It's not so easy? Sure, the transition might be a little challenging (if you allow it to consume you), but what's living if more than half of your life is spent hating your existence? You. Can. Find. A. Way. Strategize and get at it!

Spent half of your life focusing on one passion and it has

suddenly lost its zeal? Move on. Explore new passions and opportunities for excitement.

Your mom and dad want you to be a doctor and nothing less? Well, good for them! Clearly they want you to do well, and that's their limited definition of it. Oh, you hate it? Do something else. Never sacrifice yourself for the sake of someone else, even a parent. Your only chance at this thing is to look inward and really search. Listen to that little, nagging voice that you've muffled for years. What is it telling you?

Step 18

Find new ways to express it.

Discard the social norms and be ok with rejection or people not quite understanding you. Be ok with growing pains and calling your comfort into question.

There is no "right way" to live. Some people have attempted to spell it out for others, hoping to create a useful diagram, but in a lot of ways those rulebooks fail us. They keep us in the drab, uninspiring occupation. They keep us in the loveless marriage. They keep us in the stereotypical female and male roles. They keep us locked and robotic.

Do. whatever. the. hell. you. want. (Within reason, of course — we're focusing on healthy alternatives here.)

No set game plan is optimal for everyone. In fact, everyone is different and distinctive. Pick and choose what resonates best with you, but keep in mind that the more your actions work toward unification (of self to whole), the more authentic you are, and the more growth and fluidity can come to the surface.

You're floating, remember? You are operating within the world of structure, ego, and limitations, and your head is above that brooding sea, gaining access to the limitless world, open to new ideas and inspiration.

If it feels uncomfortable or abnormal to you, well, good. It should feel a little bit odd. Embracing a new way of being whilst navigating the social world ushers in a fresh mobility. It will feel different because it is.

No one has lived every single day in your human body. Others have only observed from their specific vantage points, which means that only you know the most fruitful destination, the thing that makes you want to get up in the morning and slay. No one else. Only you.

Sure, advice can be instrumental at times, but decisions are, at the end of the day, made by you and y o u alone. No one can try on your brain and think for you. No one can marry that handsome bearded fellow on your behalf. No one can borrow your body and run that marathon. Only you. Look how much power you have! Wake up and live, for once. What are you doing otherwise?

Every day of your life there will be a million and a half excuses readily accessible to you for why you shouldn't do something. If your sole objective is to lead a simple, comfortable life with slight variation, great! The Paradiso awaits you at the plateau, good friend. But otherwise: Seriously, what are you waiting for? Make the change. Live.

"I don't have enough money."

"The patriarchy crushes me daily."

"I wasn't given a silver spoon."

"You don't know my situation or else you'd understand it's not possible."

"I'll do it next month."

"Next year."

"When I'm healthy."

"When I'm fit."

"When these people around me stop doing what they're doing."

You and you alone are in charge of your destiny. You fail the moment you put some invisible wall up against yourself. What's up with all of this negative self-talk? Did Debbie Downer recruit you for her wet blanket cry club? Just doooooooo. Do it already. Do the thing. Make the sacrifices. Make choices. Prioritize and do the damn thing, lady. gent. you.

Finding authentic wholeness within the self requires a reassessment of what we've previously held as truth, amending the stale and polarizing ideals thrusted onto us since birth. No one characterization or fate can purely define you.

- Yes vs No.
- Liberal vs Democrat.
- Man vs Woman.
- Gay vs Straight.
- White vs Black.
- Rich vs Poor.

This polarization is causing humanity great illness.

The closest solution to any problem is that which brings us closer to our underlying foundation. This often means discarding the norm and structure of duality in favor of that which highlights the whole. Realizing that color is a spectrum: black and white are merely inverses of one another and could not exist without each other. Realizing that there is no top without the bottom. Realizing that gender and sexuality exist on a range. Noticing and honoring the various viewpoints. Including men in the discussions of feminism and gender equality. Including all races, sexual orientations, and gender identities in the discussion of love, acceptance, and spirituality.

RELIGIOUS DIVERSITY. BORN N BRED, BABY.

The largest question that has loomed in my mind for a while: why do some religious persons know that their belief system is absolutely the right one? For many people, the beliefs in question were merely something that the individual inherited at birth. In some instances, yes, people flock to other, much different religions. Even so, why are those more *correct*?

It always seemed silly to me that everyone just kind of believed whatever happened to be in the family. "Hey, we're Christian, so you're Christian too. By the way, we know better than the rest of the world, because, ya know, we just do."

I've come across many people in my experience who note the importance and validation of other faiths, but then make it very clear: "Yes, but I'm C h r i s t i a n." Very well then. Yes, that's awesome and thank you for sharing, but why the stark contrast? Why is the label so important? Why you versus them? Even more interesting is the difference between Christians in general. LDS versus Catholics versus Lutherans and so forth moshing it out at the main stage with Justin Bobby. I suppose identity is important to us, as it lends some sort of validation to our physical selves. It's perhaps more meaningful to put a label on it than to say *we're all kinda right, and we're all kinda wrong too.* I guess there is some comfort in thinking that our rules are a little bit better than your rules. B u t once you place yourself apart from another human (in thought or word or feeling), you are creating that same separation in yourself: to see separation between humans is an act of duality, and not operating within the greatness of abundance. To accept *all* Gods is to recognize that the omnipotent, omniscient divine could appear to us in a multitude of forms, not only the stance you have adopted as your own.

What we fail to realize is that a specific religion is appealing to us for a number of reasons. If it's a religion that is familiar (and/or familial), we're more likely to acquire it. Depending on our relationship with figures of authority (parents included), this faith may or may not be of interest. But it's not just that. Ongoing exposure to our specific culture has crafted our mind-goggles in a prominent way. Due to our own innate qualities, religion may be something that we reject for a majority of our lives. Regardless, once we have reached the age when we can rightly examine and judge a religion for ourselves, we have been exposed to a number of narratives and cultural elements that do not allow us to see said faith in an objective manner.

Mostly because objective reality doesn't exist in the first place.

Even after examining other religions (if we choose to do

so), we will still be viewing these faiths through the eyes of someone of a specific culture, in a specific location, with a specific experiential history. We will only be able to critique the new religion on the basis of the religions we've known, versus viewing them from a blank slate.

Mostly because a blank slate does not exist.

Perhaps we have had a bad relationship with that particular faith. We've witnessed its shortcomings, or participants in the church who didn't uphold the principles of the faith, thereby causing us to question its true motives. Well, we were right! Religion merely *points* to the truth rather than encompassing it entirely. If we look to the m o u n t a i n s, we'll also find God, or the Universe, or whatever fits your fancy. It's up to *us* to discover it and see the truth that lies within all things. So, too, does the religion of our family, friends, or nation at large. It's the offshoots within the physical world that distort it into something we no longer wish to practice. Unfortunately, all religions have the potential to morph the truth into an otherworldly beast, hairy moles and all.

This is not to say that it's bad to belong to any one religion. All religions serve a similar purpose and operate on similar principles. All have keyed in to the great, sacramental power that links all of life. It's just the expression in the physical world that is different. By all means, do you, boo! Whatever speaks to you is the right answer.

Step 19

Call your T r u t h into being.

NURTURING YOUR T A L E N T S

You, an individual, were given specific and perhaps varied talents and innate abilities at birth. These are one with you, or at least one with your physical body in this lifetime. In order to achieve wholeness as an individual, you must nurture your innate talents, as they have been a part of your existence for your entire lifetime. They are your nature. Your lifeblood. They are one with you. They allow you to be w h o l e. Despite any dirt and mischief pilings on, they are there with you. They always have been, baby!

Everything in the physical world is attempting to return back to its original nature. A tree reaches for the sky and yearns for the completion of its limbs, through growth, root, soil, sun. A quail joins with its bevy. A body mends its own fragmented bone. Everything is attempting *to connect fully with the greater body of energy of the universe.* The more we are in tune with our essential nature, the more enmeshed we become. Instinctually, life blends with life in ultimate h a r m o n y. Our job as humans is to look inwardly at our strengths and proclivities and utilize them for the good of ourselves, and simultaneously the good of all.

Step 20

Start with the self. Seek wholeness within yourself first, and this discovery of inner abundance will emanate outwardly. A chain reaction. A butterfly effect.

Feelings of "not having" result in more feelings of the same, and we will never feel entirely fulfilled with what we obtain. Likewise, feelings of "having enough" result in more of the same. *Gratitude.* It's not something we can simply say aloud and expect desired results. We must feel it in our fibers.

So how do we attain oneness?

Look inward.

What drives you?

What sparks your interest?

Allow yourself to tune in with your innermost feelings and desires.

Here, it's important to understand that our hopes, instincts, and intuition may differ from the collective narrative.

To backtrack for a second: the collective narrative is a construction. In other words, it's only as real as you allow it to be.

It's important to make a clear distinction between what you truly want, and what you've been conditioned to want.

If you've always been drawn to art and you wish to be an artist yourself, start producing. Spoiler alert: you might not be great at it from the get-go. Second spoiler: "good art" is subjective. Art is about c r e a t i o n and o p e n i n g ourselves to new perspectives. Yasuaki Onishi, a respected visual artist, works with a range of materials, from hot glue and metallic powder to polyurethane sheeting. Anything can be art and art is in everything. Sensing a pattern here? *Do it* already and stop letting your excuses muddle your brainwaves. Your art doesn't have to *mean* anything. Life itself doesn't *mean* anything apart from what you deem it to signify. Create. Do. Get it out there already, damnit. Once you've begun generating, you've opened a new portal for yourself and other ideas may ascend and multiply. But you won't know if you continue to ruminate on your deficiencies, will ya? Will ya?! Spoiler (x3): Not everyone will love your art. Who cares. Do it anyway.

If you're a slave to The Man, and your ultimate goal is to guide kayaking expeditions for a living, start small. Gather your friends on the weekend and curate an experience. Make the voyage memorable, something noteworthy that they can't simply do on their own, and document the journey. Maybe you'll include camping, along with the necessary gear and food supplies. Shower them in an avalanche of snacks and charge a fee. Start a social media campaign. Build a community. Showcase participants and their insights along the way.

You don't need to have it all figured out quite yet. Begin with that first seed thought and see if you can produce something in the physical world (not just your mind) to test the waters. See how it feels. Wade in it. You don't need to know how it's going to fund the private school education of your three unborn children. Not yet at least. Relax. Stick with step one for now.

Your parents may have pushed you to pursue a specific area of specialty. Let's say it's the legal field, for an easy example. You may have entertained it for a while. Perhaps you are good at debate, though you never really cared to master anything in law. You've taken on the expectations of your parents (all a consequence of the narratives at work), in order to please them.

If we're ever pursuing something strictly out of obligation, we cannot contribute to that field in the best way possible. We are earnest, compelling, and well-meaning frauds. We might appease the others for a short while, but our lack of true passion will manifest in the inability to adequately and efficiently fulfill our selected role, even if only with our energetic negligence.

Maybe outwardly we have succeeded in certain facets, but in order to truly excel in anything, there must be a marriage of passion and skill. Not one or the other. Something's gotta give sooner or later.

Step 21

If you're completely paralyzed by confusion, engulfed by existential dread, and can't figure out what's going on up there (in your brain) or anywhere else, chill out and take a breather. Use this as an opportunity to explore varied activities. Find out what resonates with you. Try a cooking class or go stare at some sea creatures. Book a flight to a foreign land. Visit a chocolate factory and gallivant through the promised land. Don't worry so much about the resolution. The process is where it's at. Clarity will come along with time and the u n r a v e l i n g. Still perplexed? You're already d o i n g i t.

You're *living.* You're simply a being in the world, lending your energy and breath to all of existence, and that's all you really need to *get.* But if most of your days are spent wishing you were doing something else, take that as your cue to switch it up and *come alive.*

We have all been born with different talents and abilities, which are all so varied that it's possible that everyone could delve into their respective intuitions and interests and we would all jointly create more harmony and connection as a result.

Unfortunately, the cultural narratives at work have made the external view of reality one in which only a small minority of people can truly feel happy or fulfilled. We see it with actors and actresses, real estate gurus, famous people of all areas of specialty. We've been told again and again (both through language and insinuation) that these are the only routes to true contentment. What we don't see is the sadness that still faces people of all ranks and wealth statuses.

The collective narrative has structured things in such a way that it at once discredits certain vocations and elevates others. Sifting through life, we are conditioned to believe that certain paths are worth taking and others are not. *This is not the case.* In fact, even the paths themselves are made up. There is no one route or destination. It's up to the individual to decide. Find an avenue that suits you and your desires, or forge one of your own. Rules are human constructs. Make your own damn rules.

Your innate abilities and fascinations will invigorate you. Cast away any preconceived notions about what your interests say about you or your pathway in life. To nurture your true calling, whatever that is, is to look inward and respect the essence of your being. You are, in a way, returning back to your true nature.

Remember that systems that exist in the physical world exist for a good purpose (much of the time) but have the potential to lose their effectiveness the larger and more expansive they become.

Think about the job market. Structure was created in order to provide some efficiency to the marketplace. Individuals were ranked for the betterment of emerging companies. Resumes were used for the sake of differentiating between candidates. School was used as a factor for measuring intelligence and proficiency. But, like all things, the system gets manipulated and distorted. People go to school for the sake of getting a job, instead of learning valuable lessons, wisdom, and knowledge. School is no longer able to provide a surefire route to job acquisition. Jobs hire according to degree and college name, versus, in some cases, hiring the person with the adequate drive and dynamism for the career.

We characterize and categorize, putting things in perfect little b o x e s, when, in actuality, an endless amount of options exists. We just can't see them with these menacing walls obstructing our view.

Listening to the advice of others can be a scam in its own way too, as most people are living according to the narratives and structures provided to them. Our parents could be the biggest threat of them all. Think about the narratives imposed onto them, and the narratives, in turn, imposed onto us. Which of these serve us? Are we living inside of the box or outside of it?

When we unpack the source of our anxiety and understand that we alone are in charge of the direction of our life, there is freedom of choice. There is freedom in general.

We still need to live in the physical world. The world of form. The world of narratives. We cannot purely abandon this like a derelict houseplant. Mostly because it's impossible. All thought structures were built through story and agreement. It benefits us and it can enslave us in the same way. We must, instead, float on the surface, as if the world of form and narratives is the vast ocean, and the wind above water is endless opportunity, abundance, and freedom. Our body can be free flowing under the waves, and our head can be breathing in the salty freshness of the passing breeze. We are suspended, seeing the benefits of the watery deep, its aquatic ecosystems swimming with captivating soft corals and the marble-eyed denizen of the sea's sheep — and utilizing the endless possibility of the air — its bounty of rich, cascading winds and silky cirrus fleets. This is balance in the world of form: understanding its limitations and utilizing its beauty and magnitude.

The world of form is not a bad thing. As humans, we possess a body. Is the body a bad thing? No. It's perfect as it is and as it always has been. A singularity and a connected part of the whole. We can only seek oneness with the world around us once we have first found this unity and beauty within ourselves. What is within so is without. The body is at once a reflection of flawless being and a sacred vessel through which we grow, learn, and become. Forever flowering.

But as we know, the ego is a very slippery thing. Once we think we've captured it and put it in its rightful place, it contorts and slips into something else. It finds a new mask to disguise itself. Our life will be constantly (and hopefully effortlessly, over time) examining the ego and seeing its many forms. We can both harness its strengths and relinquish its weaknesses.

To approach wholeness, balance must be sought in all areas of life; that means not having an unhealthy attachment to any one sector. Focus and love should be given to all: body, mind, and spirit (or whatever satisfies your preferred nomenclature). Your spirit is the constant: your consciousness and your innermost being, the part of the self that is at once limitless and a connection with all of existence. It is the essence within and beyond form. It is the truest, deepest part of us. From this consciousness springs creativity, intuition, growth, and ability. Where you see limitation, your innermost being sees none.

Creativity is not purely limited to the arts. Creativity is simply possessing the ability or capacity to create. Development in any field takes place after knowledge and ambition surrender to something larger. Creative growth can occur in any field, any interest, and does not only reflect the motivation of the individual, but the culmination of effort and receptivity on the part of the collective unit, one person at a time. Teachers create learning and depth and thought, economists create a vision of a future fiscal reality, and cashiers create a transaction and pleasant, human connection in someone's day. These are all important and deserve recognition. No task is too small. C r e a t i o n is everywhere.

A "new" idea must have in some way been built upon another one.

An author wrote a book. That book was built from ideas that were bestowed upon the author. The author could not have written a book without having read multiple other books before it. The structure of the book, or any book, was developed over time through the creative endeavors of many authors. Before the book and written language was the art of storytelling. The author had to build their knowledge to a point when authoring a book was possible. He/she/they had to go through schooling, or some sort of educational undertaking, which was a system constructed from people. The sentences of the book were built from words. Words were built from letters, sounds, and concepts. Words could not be in existence without the systematic repetition of them and a collective understanding that those specific words relate to objects and ideas. Without this understanding, words on paper would simply be shapes that mean nothing. Sounds were built from human breath. Breath comes from life. Life is existence. Every action is an expression of our shared existence. There is *joy* in that. There is *l o v e* in that.

No invention of thought or action can simply be attributed to the individual. A history of preceding brainchildren had to be born to lay the groundwork. For every idea, countless other ideas existed before it and *had to exist*. Everything you think, know, and understand has been through the filter of humanity. We owe our individuality to our collective unit and the essence of life itself.

To feel alone, and believe yourself to be an anomaly in the scope of human existence is to live in denial of our connection to all things. To sit on a couch. Live in a house. Eat food. Take the train. All indicate our energetic bond. We could not exist without each other.

Let's take the devil's advocate approach. Let's say you're a curmudgeon and a person who wishes to not be a part of the human experience at all, at least, not in the way that we're conditioned. You want to banish it all. *Let me live! Leave me be!* You vanish into the woods and make a home from the trees. You forage fruits and vegetables from the nature around you. You think *See?! I can do it without humans. Look at me. I don't need all you people.* Ol' Jim Bridger over here.

But how did you get there? Could you have arrived at the woods without being raised first? If you were an infant, left to the woods, would you not die? Who would feed you? Your deer and rabbit pals? In order to get to the place of solitude you seek, you had to first get to that astute understanding of nature. You had to learn, from many other humans, how to live. You had to distinguish between the fruits and the poison. Without other humans, you would be lost. Dead. Separated from the source. Even the knowledge of survival in the woods came from years and years of human experimentation. Think of the first person who died from eating the wrong berry. Oops. From that point on, the other humans could warn the others. Death served as a welcome reminder that nature can heal us and destroy us. At least, in this lifetime, in our physical bodies, life has been both trial and error, and you get to reap the rewards in whatever way you see fit.

Each day is a day ripe for creation. New thoughts. New ways of being. New perspectives of the world and environment around you. Each day is an opportunity for rebirth. Each second, each moment, is an opportunity to embrace a new thought pattern. All we have is each passing moment. Use it w i s e l y.

To live in solitude in some cabin in the woods is the same thing. Someone had to construct your dwelling. If it was you, and you did all of the work, how did you learn about carpentry? How did you gain knowledge to hack down the trees? Years and years of human experience, learning, experimenting, failed attempts, and successful ventures allowed for you, in that moment, to construct something. And what about the water? What about plumbing? Or electricity? Food and drink? Did anyone package the food? Who built your pots and pans? Who learned about fire and allowed you to use it for your benefit? So many things in the human experience — things we take for granted — have been bestowed upon us. They have been the by-product of a wealth of experiences before our birth. We can either honor these pieces of knowledge and develop upon them, or we can veer away from them and choose a different path. Either way, we have a foundation built in.

It's important to realize the magnitude of collective effort that has led to this moment in your life. Your ability to comprehend this information is a product of your past experiences. Learning to read. Understanding a string of words. Both seeing the words and seeing beyond them to reach a conclusion. And your interpretation of these words is also based on the cumulation of experiences you've had.

Everyone has the potential to be creative. To create.

Step 22

Think about your interests and the knowledge you've collected.

What is your personal brand of creativity? Of *C r e a t i o n?*

Creativity is being able to understand a field of information, and then look above or beyond it. Everyone has the ability to do this, but you have to be open to it. To create is to live and to ascend to your highest potential. To leave your mark in the world and contribute to the body of information and awareness within and around you.

Your creative power rests in the boundless sphere of energy surrounding you. You must first live in the physical plane amidst the body of information accessible to you here and now, and then rise above it, capturing something that has both grown from the previous knowledge base and exists outside of it. But you must look inward first. To look within is to look without. Liken the limitless capacity of your innermost being to the expansiveness of the universe. Float in the middle and breathe. And if nothing else, just be. Now. Present. That is enough.

CHEAP IMITATIONS

What we wish to seek is growth and expansion. We do so by embracing interconnectivity, glorious abundance, our true talents, and our innate, e l e c t r i c *passions*. We do so with relationships. With honoring our innermost being, our fiery core. When we honor that in ourselves, we give the freedom and permission for others to do the same. We can only authentically honor the essence of others when we see that the same light that radiates within us scintillates in the other with the same buzzing lightning flare. A dance of flames. Whenever we falter and see them for anything less-than, we deny their true nature and we deny them the right to seek it for themselves. To see their flaws is to lessen them, and lessen ourselves simultaneously.

When we align with the pure energy within us, our lives will come together, and all that we think and feel will manifest before us in complete harmony.

When we embrace abundance, our health will be filled with vitality, we will have financial freedom and security, our relationships will flourish, we will be filled with mental clarity, and all aspects of our life will be filled with love and light.

But this must be an ongoing effort on our part as well. Choose to see life in balance. Choose optimum health and mental focus. Choose balance. Refuse to surrender the whole of your identity to negative thoughts and perspectives. Choose the finely polished silver sheathing.

And alas, light is nothing without its dark counterbalance.

When we inevitably stray from our course and collapse into the depths of existential despair, let's do ourselves a solid and take it as a time to reflect and reconsider the options. Acknowledge your f e e l i n g s. Live in the humanness. We are meant to experience the full range of emotion. The spectrum.

When we choose one area of our experience over another, life will attempt to course-correct. It's impossible to over-exert in one area without another area weakening.

Say, for instance, we choose beauty and outward appearance over *the soul* and spiritual wellness. Though we may achieve a certain level of bodily health, and perhaps reach some pinnacle of aesthetic mastery, sooner or later our mental faculties will suffer. When too much focus is on the body, without consideration of the soul or mind, we will be left in anguish. Sooner or later, those once-head-turner looks will fade and the other areas of life will lag behind, sending us spiraling into some Beetlejuice-comparable waking nightmare. The severance within ourselves that we willingly construct will bring forth a domino-effect of cavings and crumblings. If not externally, internally.

Another imbalance might be focusing too much on the mind,

or the soul. For me, this was the case, specifically with being too caught up in both my inner-world and the mystical dealings of the soul. At one point, I realized that I didn't feel a true connection with my body. I saw it as a means to an end, and I never placed too much of an emphasis on physical health. I would spend days lost in thought, eating whatever, and failing to go to the gym or engage in any real physical exercise. I believed that I could rely solely on meditation and my body would somehow stay in alignment. Like clockwork, as soon as I relented to this objective and disregarded any essential forms of exercise, I got sick. With my body in stress mode, I was unable to use my mind with as much clarity and focus as I once did. My energy weakened. I realized the necessity of cherishing and nourishing the body so that all other areas of life could also be in proper agreement.

Take obsessive romantic lurve. When engulfed in it, it seems like the truest form of love, or oneness, for us. We cater to it. We lose ourselves in it. We fall head-first into this red-laden abyss of wonderment. Our partner becomes the only thing able to bring us this elevated, outward-leaning level of happiness. It shows itself as this otherworldly entity, swallowing us whole. Our mate becomes our savior, the only person capable of bringing us true joy. What a sneaky imitation indeed! "Love" of this kind is fleeting and insincere. It's not utter acceptance, but a conditional experience. It's an unhealthy attachment to an ideal. It's not love for the person, but love for the idea of what we wish the person could be. We cheapen the person, salivating on our own desires, versus allowing the true identity of the person to show itself in increments.

How do we know? When this sort of "love" develops quickly

and intensely. Sure, there are times when the connection is so true and deep initially and it ends up working out in the end, but many times this is a false reality.

The situation, at the start, results from both partners projecting their utmost hopes and desires onto the other person. We see smart and good looking, and we tack on soulmate, perfection, and the future that we will inevitably share in ultimate, unadulterated bliss. How is this fair? This person will never live up to the unrealistic expectation we've set for them.

When they act out of accordance with our ideal, we think *What happened?! It was so perfect!* Or was it really? Did we just suspect perfection without any room for error, for the faulty nature of humanity? We wonder what happened to our pristine partner, with their flawless traits falling away, when in actuality, down here on earth, this human is just as human as the rest of us, riddled with insecurities and muck and erosion.

Seeking wholeness outside of ourselves is not truly attaining it. It's a cheap imitation that's wearing the guise of completion.

Similarly, we might find cheap imitations in many arenas: money, cars, physical objects, people. Sure, they can help along the journey. Everyone needs sustenance. But the whole of us does not live in the sidelines.

We will either spend our lives attempting to collect all of our desires in dainty little boxes and, when we don't fulfill them all, assume that if we had, we would have been happy. OR, we will attain all that we seek and realize then that those things don't purely determine happiness.

Any hyperbolized focus on one area of life is an unhealthy attachment to it. What served as an essential function and a way to contribute to the world in a meaningful way then distorts and becomes an obsession. Keeping balance between heart, mind, and soul is essential in performing to the best of our abilities.

But don't fret! It's not a death sentence if we really thrive in physical health, or really dig the psychological musings of Hidden Brain, or get ultra jazzed on Oprah's Book Club, or worship porcelain figurines. Ideally, all areas should be doted on, but we'll all naturally gravitate toward one area over another. Give yourself a break and feel it out. Explore the shit out of life. You deserve it.

Living in abundance brings about fruitful results: wealth, vitality, purpose, alignment.

The illusion of abundance is also ever-present. As the ego is slippery, we must be careful of the manifestations that display only the trappings, but are not the real deal. Tricky little suckers, aight.

Wealth is one. Some people have attained wealth (and a lot of it) through less than exceptional ways: the deception of others, thievery, lies, and selfish gains. Much like the body will overcorrect for any excess in a specific area, so too will an unhealthy attachment lead to disruption in other realms of life. What may have started as a noble effort and a true expression of abundance then transitions into a gross exaggeration of it. Sooner or later, shit will hit the giant overhead fan, whether that is in a lack of true fulfillment (that comes with any desire purely felt in the physical experience), an absence of authentic relationships, or the inability to feel deeper than the fleeting emotions born of the disruptive mind.

The ego is always shape-shifting.

True and authentic expressions of oneness exist through positive thought and action with the intention of bringing about more connection, more love, more everlasting good good.

When one acts selfishly, intending only to achieve success for themselves, or a small amount of people in the inner circle, as opposed to working toward the greater good for all humans, it will falter. Abundance brings about greater abundance, whereas separation brings about fragmentation and delusion.

The microcosm is always mirroring the macrocosm.

The part is a reflection of the whole.

A sample size embodies the population.

What is true in one area is true in all.

How you do one thing is how you do everything.

And the inverses are also true.

Cheap imitations come in myriad forms. Sometimes the knockoffs are awfully close to the real thing. The slippery ego.

Step 23

Check in with yourself.

What are my intentions? Am I producing connection and abundance or selfish gain?

THE SLIPPERY E G O

The ego is the part of ourselves that clings to the physical world. It's almost like our deviant twin.

You may find solace or comfort in a system of belief. Let's call it "New Age spirituality." Through this schema, you're able to see the world, the universe, in a new light. You have expanded freedom and peace. You love it so much that you decide to incorporate it into every aspect of your life. It's good for you! It's nothing but positivity and l i g h t. Soon, you're buying crystals and doing kundalini yoga. You're meditating and getting reiki sessions. You're keeping track of your astrological timeline. You feel secure and grounded. But, you're noticing that you can't communicate the same way with some people. It's fine, they just don't *get it*. They're on their own path. You distance yourself a bit, but only because you want to be committed to your purpose. You're noticing the pitfalls in their behavior, the negativity. You're not about that. So, you get new friends. You only want to surround yourself with people *like you*. You're not sure why people don't see it like you do, but you're glad that you've found your true path.

There is nothing wrong with pursuing something that is beneficial to you, but the problem comes when we see ourselves as separate from one another, which informs a "you" versus "the other" mentality. This isn't to say that you should hang out with everyone and their mom because you are afraid of stirring the pot, but you must realize when your craving for wholeness shifts into a perspective of you being right and the other person being wrong. What works for you doesn't work for everyone else, and maybe they need to find their "thing" in time... but casting them as "the other" draws them further from finding it. The quickest and most effective way to grant oneness to yourself and others is to accept the many, diverse paths of existence.

The ego is a slippery little sucker. As soon as you think that you've controlled it and mastered it, it mutates into something less recognizable. Slips into something a little more comfortable. A sneaky, slithery thing. The moment you let it off its leash, it digs up the sprinkler system in the far corner of the garden. Oh, you'll find out but the question is *when?*

To check our ego is to first be aware of it. See it for what it is. Always be on the lookout. If we notice it early, maybe we'll need to replace a single sprinkler head instead of all of the piping too. It's the *awareness* that matters. A self-contained surveillance. A shift of perspective.

The ego is acting out whenever you are operating in the realm of duality and illusion. You're seeing yourself as separate from the whole. This is often, as our human experience lends itself to this sort of thinking and behaving. The ego allows us to learn lessons and, subsequently, advance to higher levels of being. It's a mechanism for growth.

First, we see it. Then, we make use of it.

The ego is popping up like a Whac-A-Mole at every draw. Let's try an easy example:

You're in line at the grocery store and your patience is wearing thin because you have somewhere to be. The clerk is taking her sweet time ringing in the items for the man in front of you, and you could really do without their casual pleasantries, which are altogether slowing down the process. You pit yourself against "the other," creating further dissonance between you and your fellow humans.

Was there really an issue here, or did you call one into being? Couldn't you have avoided this frustration if *you* left a little earlier? Is your view of this situation biased or inclusive?

You are always participating in your world.

There is always a contributing element, and that element is *you*.

As soon as you recognize the ego at work, you can course-correct. You may relinquish the resentment and move into a state of acceptance. The clerk is trying to do her job. That guy is trying to buy his groceries. And you're trying to get where you gotta go.

Step 24

Examine your thought patterns throughout the day.

When are you pitting yourself against "the other"?

When you catch yourself, use it as a chance to learn.

See the thought for what it is, and cast judgment to the side.

M O R E ON NARRATIVES

& the self-fulfilling prophecy

Silly you. You thought we were done with narratives? No no. At least one of you out there has a hippocampus dulled by Doritos, so in the interest of equal opportunity, I will jog some memories:

All of life we will be stuck in the vengeful whirlpool of narratives. We have our cultural, familial, national, and outward narratives that are constructing the world on a grand (and localized) scale. Then there are our own personal storylines that have been taking cues from the outward narratives as well as threading in some fanciful filigree as a side dish.

Narratives aren't bad. They purely e x i s t. They are an essential component to the human experience.

We've created narratives around our past that we are currently bringing into our present and simultaneously directing our future. These narratives can be "good" or "bad" in our eyes. Probably a combination of the two.

Our narratives instruct us to act in a certain way prescribed by them. Because we believe in their validity, we act in a way that reinforces the truth that they hold for us. We act in accordance with our established, albeit subjective beliefs, further solidifying their presence in our lives.

Take your relationship history. Let's say, for shits and giggles, that it was a sordid past at that. In fact, you've made overarching claims about men as a result. Men cheat. Men suck. Men never truly love you. Blah blah blah. You're sure of it. Even if you notice "good" men in other relationships, you are sure that either A. those men would never be into you or B. it's all a ruse anyway. Well, c o o l. You sure do have your work cut out for you, dontcha?!

Despite your desire to be with a good man, these thoughts are plaguing you and your every interaction with the species.

Now, let's turn to the present. You're meeting potential lovers and having more bad luck. Aw shit. Not again. Even if you do meet someone promising, all of your beliefs of the past are embedded in your behavior. You're guarded, wondering if this guy is going to be a fuck boi like the rest.

(Is my relationship history showing, orr...?)

Maybe the guy slips up. He's late to a date or forgets to call you back (how dare he?!). Now, you have to perfect shot to prove yourself right. See?! He's just like the rest. You tell yourself to calm down and give him the benefit of the doubt, but it bothers you. Your interactions are, to you, normal going forward. But what you don't know is that underlying energy is infiltrating the relationship in ways that you don't even realize. You're engaging in the situation in such a way that actually brings about the negative situation. Soon, he turns out like the rest. You were right.

What is it really? A self-fulfilling prophecy. You know something to be true in such a pivotal way that you're subconsciously bringing it about. You're willing it into existence! The abundance of lame dudes brings about more lame dudes. In fact, you're not even capable of attracting the guy that would fulfill you, because he won't come near you. He's too busy being attracted by the women who know that gracious and handsome men actually exist. It's too bad... but it's true. The separation that you feel with men will continue to manifest in the most unsightly and undesirable ways, all due to your perspective and your subsequent unconscious behavior. The negative qualities that you're focusing on will come to you in droves. That is, until you learn your lesson or adjust your incredulous perspective.

What you seek is seeking you.

Of course, you don't see it like that. In your eyes, you're being open-minded and thoughtful. You're being light-hearted and easygoing. But also, healthily g u a r d e d (amiright? You know who you are). What parts of yourself are you guarding, and what is that denying in your potential partner? What kind of authenticity is that? Right right... it's not. You cannot pursue something in a half-assed, self-preservation style and expect nothing but the best in return. When you k n o w your w o r t h and hold yourself in high esteem, refusing to deal with anything less than the best, you won't be attached to the false ideals of potential partners. You gotta embrace your own worth before you can attract a partner that respects it.

When you are truly yourself and operating in abundance, you know that what is for you will stay and what is not will leave. It's the ebb and flow of life. Be unapologetically you, not some cheap imitation for the sake of a fleeting romance. True, deep connections will prosper over time. If you are mourning the loss of what-could-have-been, know that you have hyperbolized its significance in some way. You have created some false future narrative that serves only your fanatic fantasy brain. That is a loss you can do without.

ESPECIALLY if you are relying on the sticky gumdrop catalysts of rom coms and social media-filtered world-views to drive your idea of what *should be*, know that you are already operating within a delusion. The narratives in your reality are as fictionalized as the ones on Netflix. All of the "characters" in your life are merely your limited scope and assessment of them, based upon your interactions and conversations. That's one small aspect of their personhood. Movies are heightened versions of the real-life narratives. They are twice removed. Discard these narratives with the same enthusiasm as you will discard the narratives that do not serve you in your own life. Be careful what you manifest, my dears.

Another falsehood circulates around our old gal, money. If you have a challenging relationship with money, listen here.

Unpopular opinion next:

If you have been telling yourself for years that money is hard to come by, guess what? It will be. Let's say the people around you also share this sentiment. Oh goodness, it must be true, right?! Well, it is for you. That's all that matters. You have not only attracted situations that propel this belief into your physical reality, but the people you've attracted as well! You've believed this to be true with such power and persistence that you won't allow yourself to see outside of the narrow window you've constructed. You cast a blind eye to all other potential avenues. Your will to be right and believe in your narrative outweighs the possibility of abundance and financial security.

Is everyone dealt the same hand of cards? Oh, hell no. Charles Edward III over here has a Royal Flush, silver spoons of caviar dangling from a well-fed mouth, and a diversified stock portfolio since the womb. Not to mention ivory skin and a rainbow explosion expressed by way of cardigan wardrobe. Marginalized folks (especially people of color) don't get a fair draw. The narratives at play globally have resulted in some very-real setbacks in the physical world. Is it *possible* to emerge and throw down some pocket aces? Absolutely. But a mindset of abundance must be present. The notion of prosperity must be readily available in the catalog of the mind.

If your life is a dire one, I'm sorry to say that you've entrenched yourself in a narrative that does not serve you. Yes, environment plays a significant, omnipresent role, but our engagement in this environment is just as pivotal. The bright side is that in this moment, you can choose to change it.

Hey, also, that doesn't mean that perceivably "bad" things won't ever happen. Larger energies are in the works, unfolding in a number of different ways. Sometimes you might be the willing prey. Other times, you play host. The more positive you are, the easier these times will get. You'll see them less like failure points and more like opportunities to pivot and better yourself. Switch it up and shuffle the deck. Perception is key. Victim mentality only comforts for so long.

Step 25

Call yourself out. Where and when are you playing the victim?

What are your self-fulfilling prophecies?

Dare to challenge your pessimistic viewpoints surrounding the following:

- Money
- Romance
- Work
- Friendships
- Body image
- Family
- *LIFE in general*

CONTROVERSY AND DISTORTED O N E N E S S

Speaking of judgment, let's talk about a controversial topic: pedophilia. Specifically, celebrity pedophiles. Very hate mail appropriate. Let's d i g in.

So.

It's easy to recline in our La-Z-Boiz and reflect on how cruel and disgusting these monsters are, right? Satan in designer slides.

First, for as easy as it can be to see through the individual and collective narratives at work in society, that doesn't mean that a lot (cough, most) people aren't playing into them. In fact, so many people are participating in the game that the narratives are being revealed within our world in very real and destructive ways.

These narratives must be at work on a massive scale for something so vile as sexual assault on minors to exist (and persist... even in plain view).

Remember Jared, the Subway guy?! Sleeper creep hiding amongst the hoagies.

When we see ourselves as outside of it, not partaking in the matter at all, we lose focus on the underlying problem at hand, which is much bigger than any one singular person.

Systems had to be in place for the cycle of abuse to happen.

First, we must note that the causes of pedophilia are unknown, but may be linked to abuse as a child, low IQ, head trauma at an early age, and other factors. This isn't the bulk of what I wish to address, though it's important to note.

Systems of belief start with great general principles and then d i s t o r t over time with more people (er, egos) in the mix; a similar thing happens with narratives and the attachment to ideals that thrive within society.

This is what I believe (sorry Christians) Jesus was (probably) referring to when he said not to fuck with false idols. Meaning, don't mistake "God" for these figures or structures within the physical world. Giving all of yourself to these imitations is very seductive and very dangerous, all the same.

So, we have someone who is making it big in the world. He's not only talented, but driven and completely committed to his craft. And yet, he is very sick (*reminder: pedophile*). Dude rises through the ranks and makes music (or other art) that awes and inspires. Jared's submarine consumption doesn't count.

(Sidenote: there isn't anything remotely jovial about pedophilia, but the topic itself is almost too heavy to talk about without sprinkling in a dash of lightness just to get us through it.)

There's nothing wrong with admiring a talent. In fact, many people have benefitted from the art. The musical gifts have served as tool for connection. The problem is when this, similar to the systems of belief, morphs into something dark and sinister. Unchecked, the brilliant, adored talent turns into a godly enterprise that cannot be contained. Fans praise and see the Artist as an entity outside of humanity's norm: something (or someone) that dictates the world around them. In fact, they don't even see the Artist as a human at all. The Artist is one with the Art. This purity. This e l e v a t e d being.

What was once a mechanism for oneness easily devolves into a strategy for separation.

The moment the Artist moves from human to God, nothing can stop him (or her).

The gross attachment to fame, power, and money takes over, shifting into a crazed and greedy beast. What started out as a pure endeavor materializes into supernatural animal.

Mind you, nothing is wrong with establishing fame, or making substantial money. Nothing is wrong with leadership and exhibiting your own talents and gifts. But they must always be checked, and checked once more (ya know, with the slippery ego in the wings).

In this case, the Artist graduates to a God-like role, surpassing all in his path. Everyone answers to him, and all who want a piece of the fame and fortune only partake in actions that please him. They allow him to act in his best (even cruel or unusual) interest, even if that interest betrays others, or their own divine essence.

And who is to blame? The perpetrator? Well, yes. Of course. Who else is to blame? The person that may or may not have abused him? Yes, of course. But what about the rest? What about the crowds of people who put him on a pedestal? The millions of adoring fans who refused to believe anything less than satisfaction about their beloved? Had he not been pronounced this larger-than-life, omnipotent figure, would he have the power to do as he pleased? Perhaps not. Not to say that there is any one person to blame, but it is all of us. There is no singular predator, and no singular victim. We're all the assailant and all the casualty, in some instance or another.

Think about this: not only is the perpetrator put on such an untouchable level that no one can seemingly dismantle, but anyone who might betray or speak up against him is automatically put into the alternative group of "people who want his money." Those who hope to out the predator are seen as either A. trying to get some level of fame themselves, in any way they can, or B. attempting to get a piece of the financial pie. An unhealthy attachment to money, fame, and power all lead to a cultural climate in which a dark underbelly f e s t e r s and feasts on its prey (many times, in unsuspecting ways).

But what if these people are, indeed, out for only the money and fame? That may very well be the case, but this doesn't detract from the central issue of false idols (fame, power, money). Especially within a capitalist society, where money is a driving force, we must be keenly aware of how the ego can alter its form and slip in wherever and whenever possible. It's always lurking in the shadows. The prevailing notion of money and fame (along with who has it and/or wants it), clouds the perception of reality in such a way that nothing can be absolutely certain. Everything is framed in this starfucker fashion, obscuring the truth.

That, of course, is a problem much bigger than the individual. It's the collective ego at work.

This is where the illusion of oneness is disguised as oneness itself. In other words: the collective unit comes together for a general purpose (whether that be the praise of a "star" performer, or something else), and it feels so powerful and real that all else is discarded. The talent of the performer and the subsequent art created (music, in this case) is confused for the person. The person is merely a *conduit*. He (or she, or they, in other cases) must be cherished (as any human should be), but not mistaken for something greater or more precious than the rest. Just as people get lost in the words of scripture, holding on to every syllable, so too do people get lost in the lure of fame and fortune. At the core, we are all the s a m e. We mistake the word for God, and, similarly, mistake the person for the art, a representation of God.

Our collective narrative has accentuated various aspects of our culture in sometimes objectionable ways. One talent or gift is heightened in value over another, leading to an excess of unnecessary attachment. In actuality, we are all given various gifts and purposes, and it's up to the individual to find these aspects within the self and work to brighten and lift them in a way that allows for more cohesion. The singer is no more important than the gardener. The business mogul is no more useful than the maid. All of these units are needed to thrive and persevere.

As individuals and the collective, we have deemed what is valuable, and we've created a sort of hierarchy of people, occupations, needs, and everything else that exists in our world. We have all conceded, in one way or another.

Money is only green paper with a portrait of a president on it. One head means one value. Another head means something else. Outside of our world, this is garbage, some flimsy piece of nothing that cannot be exchanged for anything else. It's the meaning that we attach to it that makes the difference. It's not one person, or a few people, but all of us. We all feed into that meaning because it helps to order our world. Then it turns into another mechanism. Yes, I know you already know this. This is elementary stuff. But the main point is that our culture is operating on so many of these understood beliefs that we don't even recognize them anymore. It runs so deeply. It's so ever-present that we never question. There hardly isn't even room to do so! It's a factory machine running every second of our lives.

We have carefully crafted a society in which fame surpasses all. It's no wonder our youth latch onto it as if it's the greatest cure for mankind. Instagram followers and all.

We are all to blame: each individual ego, which shapes the collective ego at large. We can only change our individual mindset in order to approach something more worthwhile for the general population.

Now, I'm not suggesting that you go to a store and attempt to negotiate with the cashier, saying that money is a lie and we're starting day one on our newly imposed bartering program. Nah, not going to work. That's not the deal.

Step 25

Take the time to see how much of our lives are shaped by the cultural narratives at large. Which serve you? Which can be altered? Which should you feed or starve?

Mechanisms that bring people together can serve a great purpose. They can also drift into a darker oblivion that keeps us from uniting.

There are tools available to us for our individual paths, but our true purpose can only be found within. The strategies outside of us may be very helpful, but be careful to not give all of yourself to any one idea, thing, person, or belief.

SYSTEMS:

WE'RE ALL DOING THE SAME THANG

Now that we've inched into controversy with the pedophilia discussion, let's just do the damn thang and delve deeper into religion and (gasp) cults too.

Are religions giant cults, or what g i v e s ?

For one, the word "cult" seems to be thrown around quite a bit. We've garnished its power in a lot of ways, alongside the smash hit "love" and notable mention "acceptance." We throw it all around like ketchup on french fries. It feels so right until it's... so wrong. And heavily ketchupped fries border on sacrilegious.

What I think is this: all religions (and many cults! *I know, I know*) are all expressing the same basic truths at their very core. The various traditions have accepted and taught this truth in the ways that have made the most sense to them. In one location and time, that truth was best expressed in one particular way. For another tradition, in another time and place, that truth was better expressed to those people in another way. No one tradition is better than another; they're all essentially saying the s a m e thing.

The problem is when this truth is confounded with the language, tradition, or elements of faith. All of these aspects of religious tradition can certainly serve a very good and *meaningful* purpose, but when the words/language/prayers are confused for the truth itself, problems arise. Believers cling to the faith, understanding it to be the only source of truth, when many routes to truth exist.

In that particular time, for that specific person, in a distinct culture, a certain faith may have been the most accessible means to deliver this truth. That, in and of itself, does not make that vehicle for truth more "right" than another.

So, at this point, we must ask ourselves: onto which systems of belief do we cling? At what point do these systems tear us apart from other humans?

The point at which a singular belief both unites people (under the umbrella of that specific faith) and separates (believing that faith to be superior) is the fork in the road where we must stop and analyze what we're reaaaaally doing here. C'mon, guys. What's up?

And hey, that doesn't exclude atheists, by the way. The relentless vigor with which atheists clench their cold, dead hands to the notion of no-God is very similar to our Bible-thumping brethren with their white, bearded Jesus (he wasn't Caucasian, folks). I'm poking fun, but the resemblance is striking. To *know* anything with that much certainty is purely delusion, to some degree. It's important to proceed with caution and know that you know nothing. Or close to nothing.

Anyway.

Forcing your truth down someone else's throat creates a larger barrier between you and that person. In humanity in general. In fact, it emboldens that person to fall even harder into their own belief structure. Interesting, eh? How about that? What you resist, persists!

And, hey, maybe all that you're reading right now is wrong too huh? I'm certainly not claiming perfection. *Take what you wish.*

There is no set structure for how things should be done. This life thing? It's purely constructed. A work of fiction, y'all! I keep sayin' it, so you gotta know it's true. The moment we decide on a rule set, that set rules us, and we're right back where we started.

Communism, Socialism, Republicanism, Democracy, Capitalism. Dazzling, I know! All of these guys seem aight at the beginning, until you realize they're doing drugs in the alleyway. Wait, Bob! I thought you were an Eagle Scout! What happened to my good li'l boy?! Where'd you get that pipe, Bob?

If you subscribe to the belief that your religion, whatever that may be, is correct, above all others, because your God spoke directly to whomever, and those very words you believe are directly the words from said God... consider: is English God's language? or Hebrew? Can anything as great and all-encompassing as God be limited to a single language? To a string of sentences? Or were those words used to communicate to a specific group of people during a specific time?

I'd like to insert a little food for thought: can we, as humans, truly grasp the magnitude and complexity of the universe? Of human life? Of life itself? Even if we claim to "come close," how close are we *really*? The species that has yet to understand a majority of what makes up the cosmos? The species that has failed to maintain the profound beauty of its home (the earth). The species that still, today, has perpetuated divisive narratives around color of skin, weight, nationality, even height. Do we really have it all figured out? If we put some rules and language around it, does it make it a sturdier base?

What if every system of belief is a little bit right, and a little bit wrong too? What if the only danger comes when we rely too heavily on the words, literature, and practices rather than the truth that lies beyond them?

Step 26

Think about the beliefs you've held for your entire life. As in, since you could remember.

Have you ever questioned the validity of these "truths"?

What if these "truths" were a lie?

Imagine what life might look like in the absence of these beliefs.

MORE ON RELIGION. SAME SAME BUT DIFF.

Let's dive deeper into the actual faiths I'm talking about:

Christianity. 2 billion people, give or take.

So, what's at the core of Christianity? Some might say the belief that Jesus died for our sins. The belief in the Bible. The New Testament. Perhaps the Father, Son, and Holy Spirit. And so on. Sure, that's all good. But what's really at the core? What did Jesus say that trumped everything else?

First, the idea of the Holy Trinity is an interesting one. God, being the all-powerful, all-encompassing entity. The son, being Jesus, who is both one with God and separate (as existing within the physical world). Of course, also, the Holy Spirit, which is hotly debated in the religious world, and subject to interpretation, with differing denominations arriving at diverse illustrations and characterizations. Some argue that the Trinity is same same, but different (laymen's terms). If the Holy Spirit has the capacity to live within all creation, including each one of us, does that not also mean that God is both o u t s i d e of us as a great, unifying entity, and also w i t h i n all of us?

God, the Son, and the Holy Spirit are all, in essence, the same thing. You, me, our friends in Africa, the dog Scooter... Jesus, God. We're all BFFs. Twinsies.

By the way, love thy neighbor isn't only talking about Marv next door with the alarmingly green, manicured lawn. It's vying for the love and acceptance of all people. Even our Islamic friends. Or our friends in Mexico who just want a little slice of the freedom pie.

Now, I'm sure I'm ruffling a few feathers here. What your, or your church's, view of God, or the Son, or the Holy Spirit is may be very different from mine. That is the power of interpretation when applied to language. That's why there are 30,000 or more denominations within the scope of Christianity. All of them, ironically, think that they've got it right.

In other news, I'm not sure that it would do GOD justice to limit HIM to three terms. Do you? If he exists as the Bible says he does, he sits up there in cloud-laced fantasy land basking in the glory of his very masculine and strangely human-if-not-grandpa-like essence. The moment we see ourselves as separate from God, from ourselves, or from one another, we are limiting his capacity (if we're talking about God in those terms, that is. Personally, it makes me a little uncomfortable).

After all... "What's in a name? That which we call a rose by any other name would smell as sweet." Shakespeare was really onto something, eh?

While I've got you here and I'm dancing in flame-worthy territory, let me remind you that I do not think that I'm right about everything. Quite the contrary! This book is as riddled with error as any other. For as much as I may touch on the truth beyond everything, these words fail to truly capture it. No words can do it justice. Including mine. Including all words. No magic configuration will master it. No amount of iambic pentameter. No poetic pizzazz. No singular entity. No amount of ice cream. Well, maybe that.

K, what about the second-most followed belief system in the world? Islam.

Islam, also a monotheistic religion, holds about a quarter of the world's population with 1.8 billion or more adherents. Surprisingly (or not!), Islam is comprised of some of the same characters as Christianity. Meaning, our pals Adam, Abraham, Moses, and Jesus all boast supporting roles in the Quran. Could it be, then, that the Quran and the Bible aren't so diametrically opposed after all? Are they both different interpretations of the same p h e n o m e n a ? Are we arguing over who said it better? Who wore it better, Christian Jesus or Islamic Jesus?

Turns out, the Quran and Bible seem to agree quite a bit when it comes to the events and figures (sharing more than fifty of the same, in fact). Of course, both books have drastically different interpretations of said events and people (which, I suppose, is where the rub ensues).

The same Jewish, Christian, and Islamic God exists in the Torah, Bible, and Quran. It's human interpretation, the desire to be right, and the need to somehow arrive at exact truth that separates us and, coincidentally, keeps us from embodying that truth, that oneness to which the texts are surely pointing.

The gospels of Matthew, Mark, Luke, and John were written 40 years after Jesus's death. I mean, can you remember what you had for dinner last Monday? What about the snack you had three months ago? There's bound to be a little bit of error there, somewhere.

For those who state that the Bible or Quran is flawless and each author was merely a channel through which God could communicate his word. Well, yes. Sure. But still, the element of language, inherently flawed in its ability to capture the greatness of being, of spirit, is still at the forefront. One could argue that those texts are merely making use of metaphor to communicate something grander.

Noah's ark? Are we trying to see the value of the message here or the structural integrity of a boat that could carry two each of all the world's animals? Fixating on the minutiae is where we falter. We must see the worth, consider the shortfalls, and proceed on with better understanding.

For those who choose to only see the historical accuracy of the Bible, please regale me with an exposé on Adam and Eve's domestication of dinosaurs.

Islam and Christianity differ in their beliefs about what God is and how he can be described. First, we should note that putting God into a singular word is already far from the truth of his absolute essence.

To limit him through the use of language is to diminish him. We should also say that to give HIM a gender is to limit him. Who is to say that God is a dude? Surely, a man wrote this. Already, we have A. limited him to a single word, and B. given him an otherwise limiting gender. How very human of us! Of course, in order to communicate anything to a body of people, we must use our very human qualities and tools in order to (somewhat) adequately accomplish anything. Language is limiting, but it's our only real modality for delivering a message (well, there are others, but still).

Can we settle on that thing about something larger than all of us being the core of all life?

For Judaism, we can rely on the above-mentioned arguments for sameness as it relates to the underlying message.

Hinduism is another popular religion, which, unlike the others, focuses on a plurality.

Hinduism begs its followers to look beyond the mind and body, arriving at the soul, or Atman. Eternal and timeless. For as different as this faith may appear to some, this central focus seems a little spot-on with the others, dontcha think? I sense a little déjà vu.

The Vedas are the most important textual works provided by Hinduism, the world's oldest religion (well, debatable). Could it have served as the backbone for future religions? Are we all just interpreting and then interpreting a bit more? The same truth lives on, despite time and endless calculation.

Hinduism argues that not only does God exist within all of us, but all things. Thus, God is all-encompassing and evident throughout all of life. Though different Gods are stressed, they are all, in essence, the same God within and without. Despite the tendency to see this as a point of differentiating Hinduism from the Abrahamic traditions, it seems as if they are all a lot more alike than people assert.

Can't we apply the same logic to Hinduism as we do to Christianity?

At once, God is apparent in the son and the Holy Spirit. Similarly, God (Brahman) is apparent in all of the Gods within Hinduism. We often cling to the idea that these traditions are so dissimilar in their assertions, when we are, in fact, just misinterpreting their claims.

God is all. God is one. God is a multitude of forms. God is everything. And yet, God is not one thing. He is everything and yet he is nothing. That is the irony of language: it helps and it hinders. It creates logical fallacies. Just as God is everything and nothing, language serves us and dismantles us.

And hey, don't believe in God? No worries. I got you:

Energy is all. Energy is life. Energy is within us and beyond us. Energy binds and breathes. Energy is e v e r y t h i n g.

Step 27

Try on for size that you might very well believe something entirely different if you happened to be born in a different part of the world.

Try on for size that all humans are searching for truth.

Step 28

Think of someone who is ideologically dissimilar to you.

See yourself in that person.

CULTS, RELIGION, INSANITY

I've always found cults to be especially interesting. Mainly, because in my eyes they look and feel so nearly identical to organized religion, but micro-sized. Polly pocket Jesus. On a global scale, organized religion has, again, worked within the opposition that exists within the physical world: at once, they work toward a greater good (connecting to the source), and they also create greater separation between groups of people. They rally and they slaughter for the sake of dominance and who *got it right*.

It's like two siblings fighting over whose mom is better.

We can look at organized religion and see that the main purpose of oneness/love is clearly a motivating factor for its members. Somewhere though, things get warped and the pure intention that once existed gets a bit h a z y. And the same goes for cults, if not more pronounced; it's all kumbaya until the leader takes a stab at playing God, forcing followers to hand over their minds in exchange for fanatical obedience.

Think of the injustices that have played a role in some of the largest religions:

- Priests who molest children.
- Doctrine-crazed followers who commit suicide in the name of Allah.
- Every religious war in history.

People cling to the truth that lies within these religions. They get hyper-focused. They ignore the questionable offenses. When more people are involved, not only do the followers feel more encouraged to turn a blind eye to whatever injustices are in the mix (hello, sheep mentality), but the probability increases that the initial purpose will be distorted in some sense without us (or them) even realizing it.

For as much as people are generally cautious about emerging cults, we should be equally monitoring the state of our largest religions and their respective players.

When people get a taste of the limitless possibilities that exist within the plane of oneness, everything seems possible. Suddenly, love encapsulates everything. Everyone, at the core, is the same. We all possess the beauty and grace that characterizes the "God" of which we often speak. The essence of being, of life, threads together all beings and living things. It's i n t o x i c a t i n g.

When people get a feel for this and experience it fully, a whole new world opens up. This is what happens with cults. At the base, they touch on these elements of expansion and love (as the major religions do), but somewhere along the way they lose their footing and stumble into a deep ravine. At that point, it's hard to get out. It's dark and dreary down there. Lost your wallet. Lost your mind. Followers are so deep in it that they can no longer differentiate between sound and unsound logic. They cling to the "truth" and believe that, if they continue to keep sight of it, all will be good.

At the core, Heaven's Gate, a fairly well-known cult, was promoting the idea that organized religion has failed us, and that the essence of humanity and the human spirit have been obfuscated by worldly desires. It begged its followers to see past the physical world in favor of something larger and more powerful. Sound familiar?

Now, the language with these guys was a little, well, unusual, what with arguing for spacecrafts and seeking a higher realm: the Next Level. In short, it was just as wacky as "normal" organized religions, but we don't notice the parallels because, over time, we've been accustomed to only accepting the religious jargon of the big mama faiths like Catholicism or Judaism. Kingdom of Heaven? Next Level? Samesies. They just threw some aliens in there and told everyone to off themselves in black Nikes.

The same reasons people are drawn to religion, philosophy, and various principles also draws people to cults. The problem is when human will is compromised in favor of the group's desires, which may or may not be favorable.

If you ever look up the definition of cult, it states that its qualifying elements are, 1. religious beliefs which appear peculiar to outsiders, and 2. a relatively small number of people.

Religious groups and cults aren't so dissimilar after all, if you account for the numerical differences.

Ever think, *Wow, kinda weird that these people are praising an elephant God?* Ever wonder that maybe those same people are thinking it's *kinda weird* that Christians are praying to a statue of a guy nailed to a cross? Kinda masochistic, no?

My goal is not to shame anyone for their beliefs. Nah. Believe whatever you want! But remember to question. Why is it that you believe whatever it is that you believe? Was it passed down to you from your mother and father? A familial thing? Did *they* ever question?

Why do we humans think that we're so right about everything? Our track record isn't the greatest. Remember when the sun supposedly revolved around the Earth? Or when the cigarette was heralded as a miracle health cure?

It has been the minority, those few outlier individuals, who have had the courage to challenge the majority and argue in favor of unpopular ideas. Sure, some of the time those ideas are not beneficial to society, but sometimes (sooooome-times) they're right on the money. Herd mentality is easy. Get those pigtails out of the sand, Cassandra. It's time to breathe that good good. That new new.

For many systems of belief (at least, those teamed with spiritual narratives), the central tenets seem to focus on similar ideas. Namely: that the physical body is a myth. We are all connected. The soul, within and without all of us, lives on in eternal bliss. Or something like that. In a way, our individuality is a lie. The language surrounding that foundational truth may be different, and perhaps shrouded in, dare I say, a colorful and utterly unorthodox quilt, but the gist remains the same. Sure, some people focus on elephant Gods, or men walking on water, or aliens in search of a higher good... but what, if anything, resonates at the core?

What makes a system of belief *true*? The number of people who willingly (or as a consequence of conditioning) adhere to it? The time it has existed in the physical world?

What IS truth?

Perhaps all of these perspectives on life and the afterlife are touching on something critical and essential. Maybe they aren't all drunken/drug-induced ponderings, the subsequent aftermath of humans locked in an otherwise meaningless existence or sipping on alchemized agua-turned-wine. Maybe the same crucial truth that has expressed itself in the major world religions has likewise manifested in smaller groups, in reckless, harmful extremes.

Now, I'm not arguing in favor of cults. I'm certainly not saying that religion and cults are one and the same and everyone's a nut job. What I mean to express is that maybe, at their respective centers, an essential truth remains: that of the soul, of the energetic n u c l e u s. But the harder we grasp, the further we get. The ego takes over in its vengeful fury. As we submit ourselves to the beauty of what lies beyond, the ego slips in; suddenly, no room remains for questioning, the notion of God (or any suitable substitution) devolves into a constricted box of interpretation, and your afternoon tea service comes with complimentary Kool-Aid.

The principles that initially bond the followers get lost in the sea of egoic doctrine, creating a force of division and splintering its believers from the rest of society. It isn't the oneness that obstructs, but the mess surrounding it, attempting to cage it in its philosophy. Nothing in the physical world has the capability of tying down the essence of being. It is far too expansive and beyond our mental limitations.

I must sidebar here to note that "cult" is yet another misnomer. Yes, small groups of people pledging allegiance to a specific purpose/ideal and disowning their non-believing friends and family is very (obviously) troublesome. What isn't so problematic is the underlying beliefs. Some of them may be a little unusual to the common eye, yeah. But dangerous? Maybe not (at least, not if they promote a common good). What *is* problematic is when the structure takes over and leads to separation. In other words, when the belief system forces its followers to disassociate from the rest of humanity in an effort to, presumably, better embody their higher purpose.

If these beliefs truly mirrored the truth of what lies beyond, they wouldn't promote discord and disassociation. Authentic ways of being, by contrast, strive toward collective harmony, not only peace and tranquility amongst its members. To live in essential truth is to emanate love and acceptance without restriction.

Just as "God" has lost its power and force as a term to represent something larger than ourselves, so too has "cult" misrepresented the groups to which it has been linked. To clarify: I am not stating that cults are dandy and we're totally misunderstanding them, but whenever we jump to label an outlier group as a "cult," we take away from what they could be expressing to the majority. We discard them, stamping them with a seal of disgrace and moving on, hoping they'll leave, ever so gracefully and silently. What we fail to recognize is how they might be s i m i l a r to us. What are they hoping to accomplish and what has been so absent in our society to drive them to these means of zealotry?

What propels these people to embrace the "cult"? How are we failing these people as a collective unit?

Has organized, large-scale religion lost its ultimate power? So much so that people on the fringes feel that the only route to spirituality is through the means of a "cult"?

When we see someone as "the other," this is another slippery tactic of the ego, attempting to keep your fragile identity and subtle superiority in check. This is the illusion. The physical world and its rule of duality surfaces. The result is two-fold: on one hand, every individual is entirely responsible for their own actions. On the other hand, the collective unit also plays a part in the atmosphere and climate at work. What has culminated in the last months, years, decades, and beyond to create the right environment for certain actions to be available and seemingly promising? When we look at an issue on an individual level, we must also consider the collective responsibility and the role that we each play. *Everything is interconnected.*

If oneness — embracing the essential, core energy/spirit inherent within all life — was accessible to all beings without the divisive excess of dogma, would the necessity for cult development exist? The state of our world is such that people feel the need to cling to the strategies of various belief systems, hoping to find the right words, jargon, and ways of life to finally unlock the key to existence. It is all around us and within us. Right and wrong only exist within the physical world as a function of the flawed mind, an extension of the human condition. Relinquishing the need for any one set structure may be our only saving grace. All systems point to our essential nature and simultaneously avert it.

For further insight on some of our beloved cults and/or baby religions:

The Peoples Temple

One of the more well-known cults, this group existed from 1955-1978 and was led by the notorious Jim Jones, the charismatic front man.

At the core, The Peoples Temple held beliefs that ultimately shared the backbone of community and humanism. Their main objective was to reconstruct the social landscape in a way that could best represent their utopian perspective, instilling renewed faith and hope in human beings, the mechanisms for change. To better represent their ideal community, they cut ties with the rest of society and set up shop elsewhere, essentially constructing the perfect environment for corruption (whether that was the intention or not is up for debate). They, as you may or may not know, ended up drinking poisoned flavor aid (where "drink the Kool-Aid" first got its hype) and participating in a mass suicide. Things surely went awry. What began as a pure intention for salvation deviated into a wicked imitation.

Scientology

Founded by science fiction writer L. Ron Hubbard in the 1950s after first publishing his book *Dianetics*, which centers on the interrelationship between mind and body from a metaphysical standpoint.

This system of belief (still in operation), focuses on the soul as a distinct entity apart from the body. In an effort to construct their own separate body of work, like most cults/ religions, they built a new language around their beliefs. Though the differentiation between soul and body is nothing new, Scientology uses such verbiage as "thetan," the term used to quantify the spiritual core of the person, outside of physicality. Well-versed Scientologists gain access to the juicier elements of the belief structure, including the deep-rooted paranoia surrounding ill-intentioned outer space creatures. Of course they gotta throw aliens in there. And Tom Cruise. (Very Hollywood, this one.) Torture, hierarchy, and harassment all come packaged in the box set. John Travolta's in there too somewhere.

Eckankar

Founded in 1965 by a gent named Paul Twitchell, an ex-Scientologist. Still going strong today. The main objective for Eckists is to be a "co-worker with God."

"The Path of Eck," as they call it, bears a lot of striking resemblances to anything you might find in Christianity, or Buddhism, or Hinduism, especially in regard to the language around God or the divine, but sometimes trading time-worn terminology for new and shiny Eck-like language (i.e. Divine Spirit = the ECK, name of God = HU). Proponents of Eckankar believe in the shared likeness between humans and God (humans made in the image of God). Then again, Eckankar looks and feels like other traditions too, adopting beliefs like reincarnation, karma, and past lives. A greatest hits album, if you will.

It's possible that Eckankar serves as a doppelgänger for other faiths because Twitchell himself has straight-up plagiarized from a number of established texts and passed them off as his own; though Eckists might counter that Twitchell was simply a "master compiler."

The Kashi Ashram movement

Founded in 1976 by Ma Jaya Sati Bhagavati, aka Joyce Green. Was (and is currently) organized by the principles of compassion and community.

Their interfaith/interreligious mission supports a "feed everyone" core tenet, which promotes inclusivity above all, as "one's own God within" can be discovered through various pathways. Things got a little suspicious when followers were under the impression that the leader (Ma Jaya) was a God, and rumor has it that followers were encouraged to forfeit their children to her. The 80-acre Florida ranch, home to Kashi Ashram was (is?) reportedly a breeding ground for accounts of beatings, rape, and other abuses.

Ma/Joyce first encountered Christ in her Brooklyn home, followed by a case of self-diagnosed stigmata and a "Christ diet" weight-loss plan that allowed her to shed 65 unwanted pounds.

The Exclusive Brethren

The original Brethren movement originated in the 1820s in

Dublin, and the Exclusive Brethren was established in the late-1840s by leader John Nelson Darby. Like a travel-size evangelical Christian secret club.

This is a religious group that disavows the "evil" pitfalls of the secular world. In an effort to achieve salvation, members disregard any need for worldly desires, including enjoyment of any kind; say goodbye to your TV, sports, movies, radio, fun, life. Like many cults, Exclusive Brethren are a secluded bunch who detach from the world as we readily know it. They see, if I am correct in this assertion, that the "normal" social environment is plagued with unnecessary extravagance and pomp. To attain enlightenment, followers must dig deeper than the shallow facade of the physical world.

But if you leave, you're dead to them.

NXIVM

Founded by Keith Raniere in 1998 under the guise of a multi-level marketing company and vehicle for personal and professional development.

Wearing the mask of a self-help seminar series, this cult lured its members in before asking unusual acts of devotion of them (branding the skin of the pelvic area, for one example). Lesser-known sectors of the cult encouraged a master-slave relationship between its senior and junior members, solidifying the hierarchical structure in place. Many of the concepts that initially granted power to its members were then used as manipulation tactics further into the series. Freedom turned to forced sex slavery. Raniere was imprisoned for multiple offenses, including sex trafficking, racketeering, child pornography, and forced labor, amongst others. Quite the laundry list.

Many cults and religions hold something valuable and true at their core. When the significance of that truth is revealed to its followers (or potential followers) the resulting bond to the teachings, leader, and fellow devotees proves deep and lasting. It's the intense connectivity, the interconnectedness experienced by the followers, that allows for such an impenetrable force to come to fruition within the parameters of the cult, but quickly devolves into chaos and turmoil within the physical world, revealing disconcerting behaviors, unhealthy attachments to the leader and one another, and a host of other dangerous manifestations.

When these small communities are exposed to this element of oneness, it resonates so deeply that the followers will do anything to keep it within their reach. This is the true danger of any belief system, or, really, anything in the physical world that allows one person to feel completely bound to another thing, person, or experience. This is the power of love. This is the power of unhealthy attachment. What begins as adoration shape-shifts into fixation.

True oneness is seeing the other as one with you. It is not seeing the other as more advanced or superior, or even lesser than. This is where the physical world distorts the image. This is the slippery ego at work.

Promotion of the connectivity between all things is expansive and inclusive. It is not limited to a singular group or entity. It is not determined by one specific modality of belief. It is manifesting in the physical world in myriad systems, interwoven through science, math, music, philosophy, various religious beliefs, and the very fabric of communities. Where we falter is our devotion to only whatever subjects we've individually chosen. We are failing ourselves and our collective unit when we discard another's belief for fear that our own will somehow wither or pale in comparison. An expression of superiority is not mirroring divinity. Such is paltry and wanting. Our duty as human beings is to give up that ghost. Allow our belief to synchronize with another in boundless fluidity. See the commonality of truth emanating in its varying forms and structures.

The interesting thing about many cults, and especially the ones that have been most publicized, is the tendency for the audience to focus purely on the aftermath. The outcome is obviously very important, but isn't it even more important to ask *How exactly did we get here*? What drove these individuals to conform to the group's identity and abandon all social norms? How are we, as a collective unit, responsible for this outcome?

The moment we think we're completely innocent, we deny the interconnected nature that exists between us. It's too easy to mark this as an outlier situation. The part reflects the whole. What we deny in the other is what we deny in ourselves.

That being said, cults can be very harmful, and a healthy skepticism is par for the course, but are we *judging* or are we *helping*? This discussion is more for the purpose of *why* cults exist, their origin point.

For the people who cannot possibly wrap their minds around

the idea of joining a cult, I must really emphasize here the profound effect that comes with recognizing the power of what lies beyond (and within ourselves). Once experienced, love and high vibrational energy seem to flow in and out of all things (not unlike an acid trip). My inclination is that, on some level, the people of all of these belief systems are experiencing that. Desperate to hold onto the limitless energy and grace, they stop at nothing to keep it, blinded by the light. The more they grasp, the further it retreats. Darkness slips in like a sinister thief, dulling the glow in a slow progression. The followers, so entranced by the beauty of light, lose judgment, individuality, and purpose. They think the only way to salvation is through these means. The ideology that provided guidance and warmth falls into a dark abyss, but the turning point was too unclear to notice —like the sun escaping the day by plunging, ever so slowly, into night.

Step 29

Join a cult.

Juuuuust kidding! Proceed with caution, but avoid s h a m i n g others with beliefs that are incompatible with your own.

PLATO, KANT, MULTIPLE INVENTION, E T C.

For centuries (and longer) humans have played around with the idea that the physical world is more than it appears. Something is beyond the realm of human understanding, and we're viewing the upper peninsula when there is so much down below for the discovering. Or at least, the surmising. The tip of the iceberg, *if you will.*

Sure, the pessimistic, nihilist, "realist" part of myself taunts the others. We're all attempting to find more meaning in this life, when in reality, the physical world is all that there is. Right? Does this a p p e a l to you?

Our incessant scavenging on the treasure hunt for truth is a defining motive for our species. *What is it? What does it mean? Why does it mean that? Who says?* The world as constant, in-flux, supposition symposium.

Plato, in his Theory of Forms, suspected that all of the physical world around us is merely emulating the ideal form that exists b e y o n d it. Meaning that an object, at its core, possesses an element (or some sort of essence) that defines it as the thing that it is, but it only serves in its lifetime on earth to approach the true, unchanging glory of the ultimate *form* of that thing, which exists beyond the physical plane. No human in the physical world is perfect, but the human form is perfect. Get it? Kinda?

The physical world is always changing, yet the forms remain the same.

All objects in the world are merely representing, in a sort of substandard way, their respective forms. Every "thing" has a corresponding, perfect form.

Perhaps this idea is most notably reflected by Plato in *The Allegory of the Cave,* which suggests that we, as people, are only able to see the world through a singular frame of reference (namely, through our limiting senses).

In the cave, people are in chains, unable to look at anything but the wall in front of them. Behind them, a fire blazes, whilst objects pass before it, casting shadows on the wall. Thus, the shackled people (aka prisoners) can only see the shadows, unaware of the corresponding fire and objects creating the imagery. In this metaphor, the objects would be the forms, and the shadows would be what we, on earth, witness through our senses. We mistake the s h a d o w s for true reality.

Immanuel Kant mused in a similar fashion regarding our subjective view of the world. His very influential work surrounding Transcendental Idealism (he made it up), suggests that our perception of the physical world is not objective in the least, but rather a consequence of our mental (and sensory) faculties. We only know the world as it appears to us. Even more, space and time may not be the surefire, fixed absolutes that we understand them to be.

Are we in the m a t r i x ?

Is this all an i l l u s i o n ?

Maybe concepts and theories appear to us as they're meant to. Maybe the human ego is the only thing shielding us from our full potential and profound insight.

Multiple discovery (also known as simultaneous invention) submits that inventions and scientific developments (and perhaps new ideas themselves) occur to multiple people at generally the same time. Meaning, ideas pop into a whole buncha heads simultaneously.

This idea counters the "heroic theory," which basically claims the opposite: that fresh ideas come to one person (the hero, if you will).

In that genius world of Nobel laureates, multiple discovery is very much a thing. A few people can be awarded with having come up with the same invention/innovation. Separate places, same idea! Almost as if the idea itself were floating in the air and happened to plop into several minds at once (the whole 'happening' tending to be into the minds of brainiacs, but *still*, ya know?).

What's an example, you ask? Try calculus. OR MAGNE-TISM. Completely different places and people, but the same development. Similar freaky situations occur in all fields, including art and the humanities.

We're talking: people in entirely different countries arriving at the same conclusions. What is happening?!

The discovery of oxygen?! Black hole theory?! The atom bomb (womp womp)?! Polio vaccine (better). Something called packet switching?!

Perhaps, though, it's not that surprising. Previous expansions of concepts and theories have both emerged and fallen away for the newer innovations to come to fruition. Naturally, more than one person would stumble upon it.

Collectively, where have we been? Where are we going? How are we going to get there?

Maybe the best route forward could only truly be stated now, with all of the past at our heels.

The invention of one thing cannot really be attributed to only one person, but to every person before him/her/them that laid the necessary groundwork. We are meant to create, as humans. To collaborate and connect in meaningful ways. And we all have the capacity to do this. If you do not fancy yourself an inventor, maybe you can be a catalyst for innovation. Maybe you are the crucial link for emerging ideas. Maybe you're not a musician, but you produce. Maybe you're not a singer, but you have an ear for talent. We all have a part to play.

Respect a body of knowledge and then seek beyond it. Open and explore. Almost like a rhythmic ebb and flow between what we know now and what we have yet to know. How are we merely reserving ourselves and how can we break through? We each have this capability.

What, socially, *is* working for us, and what needs to be adjusted?

As a woman, it's been metaphorically beaten into me: the idea that I need to advance to a certain age, mate, pop out some miniature people, raise them to perfection, die. What about the cost of badly executed healthcare, our self-inflicted planetary torture, and lead in our drinking water? Would my procreation help to ease the turmoil, or add to it?

I own my own business. I love my life. And I'm lukewarm about producing spawn. So, what's the use? Maybe variety is the name of the game and I can just, like, play it by ear. What? Too risky, you say? What if I lose my looks and the ol' tubes dry out? Get withered and diaper-reliant? Bingo my only pal? Cats as therapists?

Sure. Why not.

Toss a coin and see the chances of *'Til death do us part*. Perhaps not everyone is suited to meet the love of their life in the ripeness of 20-something, or even 30-something. It's not a character flaw, it's our ever-evolving state of affairs. Why are we all so hung up on it? Is *Pride and Prejudice* to blame?! It's not that I'm opposed, just inquisitive. I never cared for Mr. Darcy. Or any of the Brontë sisters, if I'm being honest.

Nothing is wrong with navigating a solo lifestyle, and certainly nothing is misguided about being in a partnership.

Are we upholding these structures for good purpose, or are they the consequence of repetition and tradition? Are we meant to sustain them, or move beyond them?

Step 30

Identify the stale traditions that you maintain out of habit or convenience.

How are you partaking in the collective narrative? Which aspects of this paradigm no longer fit into your authentic mode of being?

If you could do anything you wanted, what would that look like?

Step 31

Write a list of all of the excuses for not obtaining your ideal life.

Great.

Now throw that nonsense in the trash where it belongs, buddy.

No one on this giant rock, except you, can live y o u r life.

SIMILARITIES IN PHILOSOPHY AND RELIGIOUS THOUGHT (+ NIETZSCHE)

Philosophy and religious thought seem to exist outside of one another, carving out the dance floor in separate ball-rooms, when in actuality they're reaching the heights of inebriation at the same wet bar. We're all sipping on the same juice. Some of us use our newly established powers to slip incognito into the nearest convenience store for whatever divinely inspired potato chip variety reveals itself to our awoken eyes; others mutate the body into a piñata of metal projectiles. Zealots abound, wound by religion or not.

Our most enlightened visionaries have occupied different camps, from black leather jacket atheism and Camel Red Camus, to the Curly Sue payots of Hasidism. The baseline truths, which lay the groundwork for the visionaries' respective bodies of work, often expose a common thread. When the truth of oneness is revealed, there is no mistaking it. Adopting a specific God or belief system may be beneficial to some, but the ultimate objective is to look deeper and recognize our s h a r e d energy, fused into people, plants, animals, and all of life, without exception or border. To grow is to constantly re-evaluate and *evolve.*

It's not always ideal to embrace each philosophy in terms of how it was intended hundreds of years ago, but rather to interpret the messages in how they might be applied today. Like any school of thought, the philosophical notions put forth by various intellectuals are debated. And then debated more. Those within the ring of discussion will be hardheaded in their assertions, claiming that the philosophy could only be seen in a certain light.

I am claiming that my interpretation may not be correct. One philosopher's view of society may not line up exactly with the state of affairs present in our current climate. Or maybe they apply in the exact same ways.

Nietzsche's famous pronouncement of "God is dead" (which has been perhaps largely misunderstood) called into question the religious institutions and frameworks of his time. God, as personified through the Church, no longer served the purpose it once did (or claimed).

This is nihilism.

Nietzsche's unabashed denunciation of the Church and religious thought at that time lent itself to a larger critique of institutions as a whole and their pivotal yet coercive role in both the individual and collective consciousness.

Without this analysis, power remains u n c h e c k e d.

In many ways, we're confined by our culture. We're told

which brands to buy, which schools to attend, how to raise our children, when to smile, and how to stay in our lane like good little citizens. Everything is prescribed.

If we see a perspective that doesn't suit our own, we block or unfollow. If we "like" something, it multiplies to a degree beyond our immediate understanding. The echo chamber of our times is a dangerous force. Our own limiting beliefs are reverberated back to us in consistent, algorithmic succession.

We snicker and call "the other" a coward or fraud. We cannot comprehend the opposing viewpoint, because we're intentionally (and involuntarily) surrounded by only the stances that stroke our back and whisper sweet nothings. We're only courageous around our likeminded comrades. Authenticity is lost to the fabric of sandcastles.

We're afraid to be civil in our disagreements. We're afraid to compromise.

A NEW NIHILISM:

DISCARDING THE IDEOLOGIES THAT NO LONGER SERVE

All of history is essentially a giant game of tug-of-war, a combating of opposite forces. An action in one direction then counters with an action in the contrasting direction as we propel forward and attempt to reconcile the difference. Progress greets us when we have the courage to challenge the status quo, when we can assert authority and call into question some of the most popular beliefs held in our own culture: critiquing government, or our church, and other institutions with great power and force. The larger the institution, the greater the capacity for corruption.

How can we be better? A lifelong question and subsequent endeavor.

What we can do is a consistent and conscious unraveling. An undoing.

For Nietzsche, the truth was complementary to his belief in nihilism, or, at least, his brilliance surrounding the honoring of this current, present-day life, without the unnecessary reliance on an afterlife or an omnipresent deity to claim our fates.

In many ways, the nihilistic perspective has been misrepresented in culture. It's marketed as drab, melancholy, purposeless. Drenched in black eye liner and cloaked in morbid velvets.

If life is meaningless, what's the point?

But everything is left once there is nothing. If there is no objective meaning to life, each individual has the power to construct purpose and significance.

Much of my disagreement (in my earlier days) with organized religion stemmed from the Church's ironic obsession with the afterlife. It seemed to suggest that we should all act altruistically for the sake of earning back pats for our posthumous selves, and thereby gaining access to the donut-and-cream-filled heaven mixer. As in, we act now for a prize later. All of the intense characterization surrounding Lucifer and his fire fetish struck me as hyperbolic and scare-tactic heavy. In some ways the Christian moral code appeared self-serving and perhaps a little narcissistic, only tossing a life vest to those who swore to love Jesus, and Jesus alone. Was Jesus so jealous? If so, maybe he isn't who we thought he was, or maybe we're missing something here. In other ways, I was missing the point of the exercise.

Though I do tend to agree with overarching sentiments expressed through the Bible and other works, I think that any organized faith that methodically segregates and champions its perspective as superior to other belief systems loses its harmonious edge. And validity.

The same truth could not be revealed in the same ways in different parts of the world. It takes shape in the appropriate form for each group or culture.

If Jesus did walk on this planet with the intention of smacking some truth into us, I don't think he'd be too pleased if we spent most of our time splitting hairs over semantics. When we resort to the tribalistic mania of "us" versus "the other," we're not quite getting it.

It is important to fully experience human life in this physical plane: seek innovation, purge the outer layers of ourselves time and time again, and reach newer levels of awakening. When our individuality is tied to a superficial and dampening narrative (one that isn't even ours, but something thrusted onto us) we no longer have the ability to reach outwardly. We remain closed off in a suffocating bubble.

How would we know?

Our energy is low.

Each day is reduced to a mindless routine.

There is no "spark" to life.

The sparks that do exist are only the consequence of over-indulgences: drinking, eating, sex, etc.

General feeling of complacency.

When we allow ourselves to open, we r e c e i v e. It may not show up in the exact way we anticipated, or, quite frankly, may have wanted, but it will always manifest and make itself known.

"Truth" discloses itself by showcasing the colors that suit the palette of each individual. Meaning: wisdom will be imparted within his/her/their realm of knowledge and scope of understanding. If your vision is comprised of steel greys and oceanic blues, your truth will be expressed in a tone that fits the scene. Don't expect neon pink on a Wes Anderson set.

What if people could lead just and good lives, even outside of the Church's regimen?

A nihilistic effort of sorts takes a seat at the table.

Nihilism is not merely rejecting the idea of God, but the archaic, masculine, anthropomorphic entity crafted throughout the ages. If something with such omnipresence and divine sorcery dwells both within and beyond us, could we truly capture it in a single word? A combination of words? A book? A building?

Today's nihilism might reject this notion of the infinite. It might see that Truth, Beauty, and Liberty fall flat within our dire cultural landscapes. It might discard or dismount the ideologies that no longer serve us in order to give rise to the greater possibility of a more expansive sense of freedom.

This is not the nihilism that you know and love and despise. This is an undoing of all that we've become. A rebuilding in our favor. A new flavor of spirituality.

Instead of simply claiming that God (or, to put it better, a dried-out and perilous notion of God) is dead, we can go further. What ideologies, held dearly and blindly, no longer serve us? We must first start with the self.

Can we only get "better" through surface-level alterations?

A better diet?

A better morning ritual?

Better vitamins?

Better face mask?

Better movies?

Better distractions?

To reach a better self, I must marry all of me. A union of mind, body, and spirit. All components must be approaching wholeness, and not primarily at the depth of skin.

Question your ideals. Question everything.

Step 32

Delete the banal parts of yourself or your inherited belief structure and muster the courage to simplify. More noise doesn't necessarily lead to better music. Strip out some of the bass and maybe there's a semblance of a melody in there.

It was like today, at one of my favorite classes at the gym:

body combat. Stay with me. It's this absurdly aggressive class that basically models after all of the traditional (and non, I'm guessing) fighting techniques. Karate. Jiu Jitsu. Martial Arts. At some points, you're instructed to force your knee into the opposition's face, over and over, to the beat of the music — the face being constructed of neutral air in front of you. All the while, you're staring directly into the mirror image of yourself, so, really, you are your own enemy — which I guess is true in a lot of ways. Aren't we all?

So, who are you? Claim yourself:

You get burglarized. It sucks. Things are stolen. Your door got smashed in. Someone took your prized beanie baby collection that was easily going on 5 mil.

You can:

A. Take the time you need to get over it and salvage some of your financial loss via your insurance. Cry. Cry more. Get over it. Live your life.

Or

B. Take your time to get over it, which is an eternity, because you never get over it. For the rest of your days, you're a slave to your ring app, checking in to see all of the action in your neighborhood, obsessing over each passer-by, taking notes and acting as your block's detective. You create spreadsheets about Peggy-down-the-street's cat sitters and the times of each visit. You tell all of your friends, family, coworkers about your new spring line-up of pepper sprays. You get super into extremist conspiracy theories, because, well, anything can happen and you don't rule anything out. 9/11 was an inside job. Obama is a well-spoken lizard. Trump's main physical constitution is that of a Cheez-It.

All right, person B., you're coming on a little strong.

We all have an obligation to ourselves. The caveman-chic version wants us to learn our lessons over and over and over again to make absolutely sure that we got it. The more refined, slightly less primitive person wants to learn the lesson once or twice, and then move the fuck on.

What we can do, here and now, is summon the wisdom of the greatest thinkers of all time and create a sort of breakdown. No? Couldn't there be a thread here? Aren't they all trying to communicate something larger, more grand and ethereal, to all of us?

Each text is naturally going to reflect the culture and time of when it was produced. We can, maybe, look at how these messages resonate with us *today*. Like maybe when the Bible commanded that only man and woman should marry, it was speaking in a language intended for the people of that time, the zeitgeist of 40AD.

Perhaps we are meant to look a little deeper. Maybe we need to, en masse, silence the gavel and allow love to simply *be*, with ourselves and with others, recognizing that sacred bonds can *and will* exist between all kinds of people, regardless of gender, sexuality, color of skin, differing beliefs, or proficiency at pour-over coffee.

HOW TO EMBRACE WHOLENESS AS AN INDIVIDUAL

The task that is at hand for you, and every individual, is how to embrace and nurture your true self.

You were given specific gifts in this vessel of yours. You, and you alone, have the ability to look inward and express those talents to the best of your ability. What you may ask yourself is:

- What speaks to me?
- What are my passions and/or interests?
- What keeps my attention?

Go there. Keep s e a r c h i n g and excavating.

I was one of those people that didn't really know what I wanted to do. I had various interests, but no single aspiration took hold of me. When I did feel an urge to explore something deeper, I did. I delved into diverse curiosities not knowing where they might take me, but I always tried. I've never stopped investigating. Bit by bit, chipping away,

I made progress and expanded my range of fascinations, staying open to the possibilities of how those mini pursuits might unfold and manifest. When I was 23, by way of travel and what I can only describe as divine inspiration, I decided that my ultimate goal was to work for myself and author books on the side. I was enveloped by the idea of opening a bar, being my own boss, crafting my own schedule, and writing for the purpose of expression and not for the sake of making a working wage. By 31, I was writing diligently and operating an award-winning cocktail bar, the product of immense sacrifice and many eighty-hour work weeks. The struggle was furiously real, but light emanated from the recesses of the proverbial tunnel. My purpose and my passions coalesced. It all made such perfect sense.

It couldn't have happened any other way.

For some, their objectives may have been established very early in life. For others, it's much later. No path is better or worse. It's up to you to make sense of your innate gifts and inclinations and find how they not only nourish your — dare I say — soul, but how they might provide something positive to the world around you. Maybe that little donation to the masses is merely slapping a smile on and showcasing a bit of joy and good sportsmanship in your day-to-day experience. Maybe it won't occur to you today or tomorrow. Just be open to receive. Challenge the social norms and see how you can contribute in your sterling, utterly individual way.

You, on this planet, in this century, on this day, with that fine-ass anatomy, full of tissue and bone and heart... you are necessary. distinct. u n r e p e a t a b l e.

For several years, I kept seeing triple and quadruple numbers everywhere I went: on clocks, on receipts, license plates, basically everywhere numbers reside. I paid attention to these patterns, not really understanding their sudden, mysterious emergence or significance. They were a reminder to keep honing in on the fruits of my intuition. I decided to be unapologetically me. I discarded whatever unspoken social contracts may have otherwise played a role in determining what I could do with my life. The more I tuned in and honored my genuine nature, the more my talents shined. I allowed my personality to shimmer authentically.

When I eliminated all of the bullshit surrounding what I could or should do with my talents and passions, a whole world opened up for me. I could be honest and vulnerable with myself (and by extension, with others). I could be true to myself. I know, it sounds like some cheeseball's guide to life, but all of those expressions exist for a reason. At the core, there is truth. I don't mean "be true to yourself" in a way that exaggerates the qualities that make you a real, true asshole. No. We're talking about some m a g i c.

Step 33

Highlight the gifts that allow you to connect with others and create a space where not only you, but others around you, can flourish.

How can you connect to the whole?

How can you, through your completion, help to complete others?

Only then will your talents be used for the creation of depth, warmth, and vibrancy in our world.

PSYCHOLOGICAL EGOISM AT WORK

One might even argue that literally everything you do is in your own best interest. This is psychological egoism at play, a stance that asserts that no matter what you do, you're always acting with yourself in mind. You ate those 200 ice creams to make yourself feel good, and you fed the homeless to make yourself feel better too. At the crux, you're looking out for number one. Of course, some actions might tip those ever-loving scales a little more than others.

If this is so, then wouldn't we want to engage in the kinds of behaviors that will yield the best, most lasting rewards? Everything you do benefits you in some way. Everyone is constantly acting in such a way that benefits themselves. We are all attempting to "become whole" at every waking moment of the day. Now, the difference here is that some actions yield short-term wholeness and some yield l a s t i n g wholeness. Sort of like we are either short-sighted or far-sighted. The objective being 20/20 vision, and not purely in hindsight.

Let's take your holiest friend, Barb, the one who looks out for everyone else. Selflessly, Barb, like a martyr, puts herself last every time. We won't get into the problematic portion of this, which clearly points to some low self-esteem issues for Barby. Within the scope of egoism, Barb would still be doing something in her own interest. What, you ask? The feeling of caring for her friends. Getting kudos with the big boi upstairs, or, alternatively, winning a dark ripple wave of delight and cheer from her satanic sisters (we would hate to assume that Barb praises one and rejects the other). We can't surmise what Barb's religion of choice is, so use your capable and far-reaching imagination. Thus, Barb is somehow serving herself by (hopefully) solidifying friend-ships (at least, in her eyes.)

Let's say a few years later, Barb turns a new leaf and really comes into her own. She has a few a-ha moments and joins a sex cult. She's ravenous and unhinged, quite frankly, swing-ing to the very other end of the spectrum (and swinging in other ways, too. huh, Barb?!). K, so, to make up for lost time, Barb really goes for it. She spends her entire life's savings on new, prized possessions, including $10,000 worth of Golden Girls' schwag. She takes trips to the Bahamas. Buys a few boi toys. The whole shebang. She's over the days of being everyone's pet friend and certified door mat. Now it's ME ME ME according to Barb, our dear friend. Now, Barb is also acting in her own best interest. Sure, outsiders might see that blowing all of her cash on sitcom schwag isn't the best move ever, but we support her nonetheless. For Barb, this is what she sees as making her whole, for the m o m e n t at the very least.

Now, the most lasting efforts to produce wholeness are those that benefit you and the other. In Barb's case, she went from one extreme to the other. Ideally, Barb would act in a way that looks out for numero uno (herself) as well as her core group and others outside of it. One shouldn't be sacrificed for the other. With balance, Barb wouldn't be so quick to overcompensate. For both the first chapter of Barb's life, and the second, she was thinking short-term. When she was solely doing things for others, she wasn't considering the long-term effects of neglecting herself. Similarly, when she catapulted herself into her hedonist binge, she was cutting off her social circle and, really, forming an environment where her BEST interests are put to the side in favor of short-term gain. The question Barb should always ask herself is: *What is this action doing for me now, and what is it doing for me ten, twenty, fifty years from now?* Cuz, like, we like that brownie today, but if everyday is TREAT YOSELF day, we're gonna be blobbin' around real fast. See also: unmotivated, tired, addicted to sugar, in poor health, etc.

Sometimes loving yourself isn't eating the brownie and giving yourself a sugar spike. Sometimes loving yourself is considering how your present actions will forfeit some of your longer-term goals, if repeated consistently.

Now, do this with love and acceptance. As someone who has had constant issues with body image, I can attest to this one. It's not always a breeze, figuring out the puzzle of who you are and what you need to head toward fulfillment (in fact, it's a life-long endeavor, so buckle up). It's easy to resort to wishful, future-forward thinking: *Oh, I'll love my body when I lose ten pounds.* But that shame can easily turn into starving yourself or restricting your meals, which in turn backfires and sends you into an escapade in which you devour 17 burgers and a milkshake. Sometimes loving yourself means taking that bod to the gym and giving it a run for its money. Sometimes it's relaxing on the couch with a good documentary. Sometimes it's doing the dishes. Love doesn't always translate to chocolates and going out for whiskey sours with the girls. Then again, sometimes it does. Doing something for the long term usually isn't the cheap thrill that presents itself to you in every passing moment.

Step 34

Let your intuition take the wheel.

What do you really *need*? What has your innermost self been begging of you?

Take a stroll on the middle road. You know, the Buddha thing.

Balance. Patience. Persistence.

And when in doubt, *just be*.

TRANSCEND THE BULLSHIT:

EVERYTHING IS MADE UP
CONSTRUCT YOUR OWN LIFE

What is essential to understand in order to transcend the bullshit is this: everything is made up. The rules. The social norms. The regulations. The way you wear your clothes. The social niceties. The *Hello, how are you?*s. Every single thing. The way you think and the way you behave is, in large part, crafted by other humans. It's passed down in this complex, unspoken (and sometimes spoken) way.

First learn this, then t r a n s c e n d. It's never possible to completely disengage from this element of society. The way you think today has been shaped over years and years of conditioning.

Text books, the language and behavior of those around you, your bosses and coworkers, the ad on the billboard, the swimsuit model on the magazine, the subliminal messaging of body language, religious propaganda, the exposure to aisles of makeup and beauty products, the news, the commercials, street signs. It's all directing you in a very specific way. It's making you think and feel and act in an "accepted" way. We all know this on a superficial level, but we fail to grasp it in its penetrating entirety.

When you consider that in order to do anything, you need to have the support of other humans, you want to act in a pleasing and acceptable way. Right? No one wants to be led by a loner. But what if more of us broke the mold and allowed for a difference of opinion? What if the largely accepted norm slowly faded away for a new framework?

So what does that look like?

Acceptance of ourselves. Acceptance of others.

That means: Not rejecting others for thinking in different ways. Allowing for diversity and freedom of thought. Not shaming someone for exposing a belief that differs from our own.

Evolution, at this stage in human development, is dependent on the movement toward acceptance of the whole. The variety of people and ideas coming to the surface and showing face. The movement from duality into multitudes, and beyond.

This kind of transcendence requires a severance with outdated, tired identifications of race. of sexuality. of gender. of human beings. We are behaving at our most primal and ignorant states when limited to dichotomies: white versus black, gay versus straight, man versus woman. Approaching oneness means welcoming the range of experiences accessible to us and purging ourselves of superfluous qualifiers. We are not defined by color, our femininity or masculinity, or whom we desire. To categorize is to define and l i m i t. Tiny little boxes.

For as much as you may or may not despise/loathe organized religion, we must also realize that the religious indoctrination that rules some is the same damn thing as the ideologies that rule our own lives. But those ideologies may hang onto us so close to our chests that we've forgotten they're even there.

What kinds of ideologies rule you?

- Men are assholes.
- Women are manipulative.
- I am bad at _____.
- I'll never be _____.
- My only talent is _____.
- My parents are tyrannical and overshadow me.
- I'm destined to be alone.
- All of my relationships are toxic.
- Rich people are selfish.
- Friends are never consistent with me.
- I'm the only one who tries in my relationships.
- I'm not smart enough.
- I'm not worthy enough.
- Only beautiful people get what they want.
- I will never succeed.

On and on and on, we've told ourselves these stories. Perhaps a few things have happened to you that have painted a clear picture about how things are structured in the world. You've had some bad relationships and now you assume all relationships will end poorly. Or, you've had some hardship around money and you think that you are destined for a life of poverty. Maybe you were made fun of as a child and you think the world is out to get you.

How are you crafting your environment? Is it a kind world or a disempowering one?

You and you alone are in charge of your perception. Yes, certain beliefs and customs have been forced onto you. Yes, you were raised a certain way. Yes, certain things have happened to you.

But how are you going to go forward now? Do you want a future in which all of these things define you? Are you willing to relinquish your control? Or are you brave enough to take inventory and only hold on to the beliefs that serve you?

Whether we want to confront this idea or not, we all adhere to our own beliefs and ideologies. These ideologies aren't strictly restricted to politics, religion, familial relations, and all of the things that we equate with our tried-and-true sense of the world. Our ideologies are wide-ranging and deep. Who do I think I am and how do I relate to others? What is my purpose? What stories do I tell myself and why?

Chances are, these stories aren't always so sweet. The voice in your head might not always have that buttercream tone. It might be:

- Wow, I look tired and ugly today.
- I really shouldn't smile like that.
- My talents are pretty subpar.
- I would love to accomplish this goal, but someone better will beat me to it.

It's interesting, that little voice inside of our heads. It's telling us some deep-rooted beliefs about ourselves.

You want to alter your appearance to satisfy some ideal you've created for yourself. Is this ideal strictly your own or did someone or something insinuate this for you? Do you have an underlying belief that others would find you more attractive if you changed your body?

Who are we trying to convince here? Ourselves, or someone else?

Consider this:

If you're operating in the world guided by the belief that you're not as attractive as you should be, all of your behaviors (conscious or not) will be tied to this belief.

You don't have the courage to talk to that attractive guy over there, because why would he find you attractive?

Or

If that guy happens to talk to you, you hold yourself in a way that seems unworthy.

Or

You're sheepish and afraid to act in a way that is true to who you really are.

Is it not possible, then, that the guy over there isn't attracted to you, because, well, you're not confident? That handsome, good dude is actually looking for his equal. And, well, you're not it, because if you were, you would be operating on his level?

Self-fulfilling prophecy, boys and girls! Here we have it.

And it's not your looks that keep you from your destiny. It's your firmly entrenched insecurities. That flat butt ain't it, honey. Those lips aren't your fall from grace. It's your shitty belief about yourself.

There's nothing wrong with analyzing yourself, but do it constructively. When you look at yourself and see something that you find unappealing, your next thought could be: *What* is driving my thought of feeling less-than? Versus: *How* do I fix my inherent flaw? You are not flawed, you've just been through some shit, and it's time to release it.

The only reason you have arrived at the conclusion that you're deficient or inadequate is because you're measuring yourself against some other standard of what you *should be*. According to whom? The masses? The internet trolls? Cool, so you're going to let your self-worth ride with the shadow puppets of the world wide web? Standards are all made up, remember? *You* get to decide.

Step 35
Create your own damn standards.

WHAT ABOUT M E (Y O U)??

We've discovered that most (if not all) of our lives are spent within our little self-indulgent movie. Everything is about us. We make someone's poor mood about us. We make the armchair warrior's comment about us. We make the rush hour traffic about us. Everything is inconvenient for us. Everything is seemingly a trigger for us. Me me me.

It's counterintuitive to realize that a personal attack on you has little to nothing to do with you. In one sense, yes, the remark is targeted at you, so clearly you have something to do with it. What isn't clear is the motivating force behind the comment. People at peace with themselves and their environment ("WOKE" people) do not spend their time degrading others. Why would they? Why would a secure, confident individual need to size up others in a way that shows a false sense of dominance? The interaction-by-interaction power struggle is an incomplete and inferior way of attempting to reach wholeness.

When you see someone as a part of you (rather than outside of yourself) you recognize their pain and relate to it in a way that provides the essential empathy to operate within an awakened state. When someone acts with anger, you notice the pain that creeps from beneath. The anger is a mechanism to alleviate some of the pain, and you are somehow acting as a trigger for them. It's not a b o u t you. This person has deep-rooted pain that hasn't been addressed fully, and it's manifesting presently in ways that seem to be concerning you. It's your job to recognize this as pain and not simply anger in reference to who you are as a person. You might be thinking, *Well, why is that my problem? That's their fuckin deaaaaal, bro.* Right, it's their problem and you're only worsening it by adding more negative juju to the mix. Chill. It's not about you.

When you are acting out in anger, you're doing the same thing. There is something unresolved, lying in the depths of you, waiting to be healed.

When one person is thinking *What about me* and the other person is simultaneously thinking the same thing, we have an issue of separation and misunderstanding. Oneness approaches this situation from a standpoint of *what about me AND them?* It's not a discarding of the self, but an inclusion of the other. Any imbalance favoring one or the other is missing the mark.

Perceived separation can occur on a micro-level (person to person interaction) and on a macro-level (larger groups encountering other larger groups, such as countries or cultures). The notion that one country or culture is better than another is merely a misguided pattern of thinking as a result of conditioning — a pattern, I might add, that brings more conflict and discord into an already tumultuous global climate. Recognizing the faults or missteps of another collective unit without internal group reflection serves as a deflection tool, a convenient distraction from our own shortcomings. We're all playing our roles and we're all contributing to the world stage, if even by inaction or blissful ignorance.

Step 36

Identify your trigger points, what angers you.

Look deeper: What do you fear? What do you repress?

OUR ILLUSORY VIEW OF LIFE

Not only are we born with individualized dispositions, which color our world in a certain way, but our particular experiences, social setting, and cultural backdrop all play a part in how we see and navigate our environment. Every physical object acts as a symbol, and you may or may not be aware of the significance of each.

You may see a man and automatically think in terms of *danger* or *sadness* or *love*.

Or see an evergreen and think *beautiful* or *paper* or *climate change*.

Or money: *evil* or *power* or *desire*.

Everything in our little world, our mini mind-space movie, comes with a code and cloaked in bias. Every moment, we see, we sense, we judge. We perceive phenomena and place each mental item into its specified box, as per our life-long saga of constant conditioning, a survival tactic we've created for ourselves to build up walls and stay safe. Keep cool. Stay outta the gutter.

This is us being human.

The only way to puncture these walls is to deconstruct them. Burn 'em d o w n, baby!

Like you might reject the ideologies of various religious traditions, you may also see and dissect the ideologies you have about your own life, your world.

Christianity asserts that the world exists for a certain purpose, backed by a story that has been told throughout the centuries. This story informs the relationship between humans and the deeper reality beyond them. You've also been telling yourself a story based on your past history and how you've related to the physical world. Both of these stories are open for interpretation.

You're choosing to interpret your life's events in whatever way suits you.

Was the lost relationship a cause for you to abandon love? Or was it an opportunity for you to learn a lesson?

Was your house burning down an opportunity for you to lose faith in humanity and crawl deeper into a victimhood? Was it an opportunity for you to see the true value of your relationships over physical objects?

Have you been using your life's events to move closer to wholeness or deviate further from it?

We can either empower ourselves or play the victim. It's our choice, and our choice alone.

Step 37

Rewrite your history and memories to reflect your growth, not your victimhood.

WE'RE ALL CARTOONS IN A CARTOON WORLD.

PLAY HOW YOU WANNA.

We get further away from ourselves and our inherent destiny (or whatever you might want to label it) when we acquiesce to the normative world. "Reality" appears to us as a seemingly objective and conclusive element of our present physical experience.

Already, we are playing a character. We are the actor. The sister, the aunt, the mother. The friend, the lover, the villain. Through the many eyes of this world, we don many hats. In this way, we are always once removed from our essential nature, something that is much deeper and expansive than any one label or combination of such.

Not only are we always already characters, but we remove ourselves again in the interest of taking on the role of the low-level celebrity. I'm talking social media. We limit ourselves to a box. We throw a filter on it. Put some cute words on it. Pray for likes to validate our cinematic, overly curated selves.

We check our phones and our various social media outlets ad nauseam. Compare our "stories" to others'. We start to think that the social media world has some upper hand on the other, less-applause-driven external situation we've got going on. Somehow life itself seems a little more empty. We post more, get off on the likes, and do it all over again. The f i x. The dopamine.

When we're not doing that, we're pouring ourselves into the fake lives of sitcom stars. Or maybe worse, the "real" lives of reality TV stars. Somehow we get engulfed by the fictionalized portrayal of another person's life. And then we compare again! Why is my life not like these fake lives?! Why do I need to take out the garbage?! Where is my servant?!

Or we delve into video games, or sports, or movies, or books.

Nothing wrong with any of these. They all have their place and time. What we might want to do, however, is take a bit of an inventory. How much of my life is being spent in the here-and-now. And how much of my life is playing out in the once- and twice-removed existences?

When do you really feel alive, full of e n e r g y and completely taken by whatever it is that surges through you?

Already, we are being programmed in innumerable ways. Your phone listens to you and delivers ads that are compatible with your daily discussions. You see images and texts that reinforce your beliefs and opinions. In some ways, many of us are coming together in our shared beliefs. In other ways, it is creating more polarization. The greatest gift we can give ourselves is love. Love your neighbor with whom you have

1,000 things in common, and, even more importantly, love the neighbor with whom you can never quite agree.

The goal is not to convince the other person that we're right and they're wrong (mainly because "right" and "wrong" are simply products of duality and do not exist as absolutes); it's fostering a mutual respect and hopefully coming to a middle ground. Or perhaps not. Perhaps it's just not killing the other person. *That could work, right?*

Shoving our opinion down someone's reluctant throat really doesn't do anything but cause anger and possibly some cruel and unusual indigestion. Calling someone an idiot for holding a belief that doesn't circulate in your personal rolodex serves very little purpose aside from cementing your ego in place.

If a large population of people is in agreement about a certain action that you deem unsatisfactory, the reason is probably not that they want to be black-hearted and return back to the dark ages of guillotines and body stretching. It may appear that way, sure. But appearing a certain way is relatively baseless. If I see a person as selfish, it doesn't make it so. I am projecting onto that person and choosing to see their actions in a very specific and *self-serving* light. Choosing to have compassion for the other person and trying to see from their perspective is the only way to individual freedom. Sure, it's hard. It's h a r d as hell. It doesn't mean you need to agree with them. But let's keep the name calling out of it, because it makes us brutish and catapults us at least 100 steps in the less desirable direction.

Step 38

Keep the elements of your personality that shine and bring out your greatest qualities.

For me, my sense of humor is something that has not only helped me over the years, but it's something that I thoroughly enjoy. I love sarcasm and poking fun at the absurdity of life. Cats in pajamas: charming. Dude hauling ass on a Wiener-mobile: funny. Guy with an un-ironic Monster Energy tattoo on his face: more concerning, but also entertaining. Woman surging with joy about stamps: a pure delight.

It's less about mocking the individual specifically, and more about how interesting and ridiculous we humans are. In the grand scheme of things, nothing really matters. We all die, you know? We leave this place. We can either have a fucking great time, or, you know, take ourselves goddamn seriously and stress the fuck out. Seriously. Do the thing. Eat the damn ice cream. Get on the plane. Leave the job. Tell her you love her and wanna have her baby dumplings.

REDISCOVERY

Abandoning the ideologies that do not suit you allows for a rediscovery. You are now granted the freedom to do and think whatever you want, without the heaviness of what you think you *should* do.

Who says?! A bunch of other people, that's who. Other people who also, coincidentally, lived their lives and made it up as they went. There is no real and true way to be. The closest thing you'll get to truth is what you s e e k inside of y o u r s e l f.

Ladies, if you're hung up on the whole ball-and-chain nuptial thing, consider the fact that marriage for the purpose of love is a relatively new concept (circa 18th century). Prior to that development, the life-long shackles were a survival technique. Financial welfare. Power and subordination. We're finally at a place where we can *choose*, which wasn't really a thing for our girls of yore. We are privileged to explore singledom and live entirely on our own terms.

A man does not define your life.

Happiness does not come in the form of another person.

If your life is unfolding unlike the people around you, good. It's meant to do that.

There is no official, unbiased rulebook for this thing.

That being said, maybe you are meant for marriage and kids, the "good life." Maybe you're cut out for an open relationship. Or a slew of short relationships. Don't let a magazine article fool you into thinking that any one romantic (or otherwise) pursuit outvalues another. Those authors don't know the secrets to the universe any more than you do, but they do know how to write stories that sell.

In the age of social media and the overflow of information, we're skimming off the top and pretending to know more than we actually do. We read a few excerpts and morph into armchair antagonists. We absorb our knowledge from Facebook and Instagram. Copy and paste from a friend's post. Contribute to our own echo chamber. Our beliefs are reinforced time and time again based on our clicks and "likes." A treacherous whirlpool.

We tend to ingest news articles that fancy and mirror our own beliefs. Even when we account for algorithms that reinforce our ideologies, we still tend to read the articles that suit us versus consuming a mix; this is confirmation bias in its true and delightful form. We are not objective creatures, but we must realize this about ourselves to really get anywhere worthwhile.

The data "truths" that surface within magazine articles are often times misleading and provide curtailed information. I mean, can you blame them? Our attention span has a half-life of negative two seconds. Convincing readers to look at the original study, and attempt to read the whole thing for clarity would be like asking a monkey to do the splits, an outlandish and unusual request. Some sources are surely better equipped than others, but all are prone to human error.

People turn to the news, or a dedicated station or publication. All lean in some direction, either left or right. What may appear as nonpartisan information really isn't so. Perhaps data surrounding an issue is correct, but the language used to represent it expresses a bias. Language, tone, body language, enunciation, debate. It's not only what's being communicated, but the delivery.

- Was the study done fairly?
- Who was conducting?
- How large was the sample size?
- How clear were the questions?

I think we all remember the wildly inaccurate 2016 election polls.

How many times have you blindly believed a "fact" that was told to you without really checking in with the original source, even if from a trusted news outlet or friend? Sometimes, it's not so easy. It's more convenient to sit back, spread the factoid, and forgettaboutit.

Some people do the due diligence. Props! I can't say that I'm a saint myself.

We need data sets, analytics, math, technology, medical research, and all of that jazz in order to advance our society, and our world, but we're amiss if we allow it to overtake us, silence our intuitive powers in favor of hard numbers and monetary gain (which, you know, is a defining factor in our country's structure).

Consider global warming. Much scientific information backs the claim that we're destroying the earth, paired with other information available to the contrary. Let's say you're one of those people who deny climate change. All right. But, using your intuition: don't you think it might be an interesting idea to take care of the planet anyway? Even if it's not dying as fast as people say it is? Shouldn't we still want to put a little lovin' into it? Like, what's the problem here? You like dirt in your soup?

What is right for the collective body (and future generations) and how do we get there? What systems are in place, and what programs could prosper? Not only theoretically. Not pie-in-the-sky hopeful.

Clearly, there is a problem if we say *screw it* and turn off the news. Crawl into hibernation and refrain from gaining any new knowledge. Hit the snooze button on our brains. And I'm for sure not saying to do that. But this external world that is presented to you — convincing as it may be — is not the whole picture. We see only one leaf of the garden. True progress is on the other side of ignorance, where we realize our inevitable shortcomings, individually and as a unit, and dare to see through the façade.

WE DON'T KNOW MUCH OF ANYTHING.

So live your life. Do yo thang.

Seeing as there is no objective reality (as we are only able to experience the world through our very subjective, human vantage point), we then arrive at the fact that anything we "know" is purely through our limited filter. There are plenty of things (we guess) that are beyond the scope of human perception and understanding. After all, you can't step out of your very human brain to experience, well, anything.

Let's take dogs for example.

Yes, we can tell when they're happy, right? They greet us at the door, wag their tails, and slobber all over us. Pure bliss. Sure! They're h a p p y.

But what is a dog's happiness, really? Is it like human happiness but merely experienced through the dog? Or is a dog's feeling of happiness entirely different than ours? There really is no way of knowing. We project our understanding of joy onto the dog because it's the only way we know how to relate. Until we spend a day in a dog's furry suit, we won't really know for certain.

We do this a lot, humans. Making it all about us and what we think it all means. We're probably kinda wrong about a lot of stuff. In fact, humans have been, historically, wrong about, um, most things.

The facts of today could quite possibly be the factoids of t o m o r r o w.

We believe things that we read in books, or happened to hear from a friend or a relative, or stumbled upon in the morning news. Much is not substantiated, yet we believe, and we cling, and we argue and engage in this nuisance game of who is right and who is wrong. We're all probably a little bit right and a lotta bit wrong. So, what now?

Aside from the expanse of the universe and the interconnected nature of it all, we really don't know *much*. We can guess and surmise, but we're pretty much left to our devices. If you really remove yourself from the mental mix, we're bundles of energy existing on a giant sphere.

Marriage is made up.

Getting a 9-5 and doing the "adult thing" is made up.

Procuring a nuclear family is made up.

The rules are made up.

Social constructs are made up.

It's all pretty much fuckin' made up.

What if, though, you challenge me? A duel!

You say if we know nothing, we can't even know about the interconnectedness of the universe! A-ha!

Ok, sure. Then we don't know.

Now what? Whatcha gonna do?

Live your life? Is that all you can do?

Is that all ya got?!

We know nothing. It's all made up. Live that life however you see fit.

End game.

Hey, if you want to make minimum wage and eat cardboard out of a treehouse for the rest of your days, do that, man.

Want to make a billion bucks and save the planet? Do that! Yeah!

Bike ride around the globe and make string cheese puppets? By golly, get at it, sister!

Go ride spaceships with your alien buds? Go for it! But, like, be careful, brah!

I mean, yes, do as you will, but know that your efforts will always not only impact you, but the people around you (and the people beyond even them, and beyond). Ripple effect, you know. Doing better for you and simultaneously improving upon the lives of others will benefit the whole. Reciprocity, bb.

Step 38

You know you're the narrator of this thing, right?

You have the power. Live it up!

SELF·WORTH

Even as a child, I forecasted the dire fate of my forthcoming love life, as if some predetermined existential lesson was built into my storyline; I instinctually knew that I wasn't going to make it as cupid's favorite target. My arrows were on backorder.

The melodrama ran deeeeep. So many sands in hourglasses.

In most of my relationships, something seemed amiss, like a part of me was hidden in a safe and my partner forgot the combination, or never cared to learn it. Not that I was a peach either. My poor self-esteem paired nicely with boys who learned some next-level choreography around the topic of commitment, complete with the quintessential pop-and-lock avoidance tactic starter pack. "What are we?" *pop-lock-pop. Sorry, can't quite make out what you're sayi— lock-pop-lock.* Ironically, none of them were great dancers. But, nonetheless, I chose to stay and consequently suffer.

I spent a lot of time trying to find my worth within another person, as if he could end my search and carry me back home. Most of the time it left me worse off. My sense of self plunged into treacherous waters whenever my ideal wasn't met (which, you know, was often considering the voyage to an unobtainable Elysium with a person who is simply not right for you). You know what I'm talking about? Building houses out of marshmallows? It's exhausting just thinking about it.

After a three-year relationship, followed by a two-year relationship, and a smattering of brief flings, I decided to take a full step back and focus purely on m y s e l f. Before that time (and basically since the time I was first infected by cooties), I always thought of relationships as a way to complete myself. If only I found "the one," everything else would feel easier and more serene. Life would come to focus.

I investigated myself in the fashion of a private detective searching for a cheating spouse in the lovelorn cabins of the seedy Motel 6, blacklight on floral duvets. What would I uncover and how shrouded in disease would it be? Hovering a magnifying glass over my early childhood years revealed the origin points of many of my habitual tendencies and ways in which I approached the world. A deep-rooted unworthiness permeated my adolescence and seeped into my life thereafter. I was attempting to undo my perceived failure by establishing my value: acing the test, winning the boy, detaching from the emotional unrest. All acts were surface-level fixes, like shoving in earplugs when your neighbor is bumping some hardcore bagpipe-screamo hybrid from his murdered-out PT Cruiser. Everything mellows a couple levels, but nothing is truly eliminated. And it's forever etched into the recesses of your mind.

I threw myself into a range of different strategies for self-improvement: the magical essence of yoga and reiki energy healing; time-warping tarot and palm readings; crystal healing and shamanic journeys to other astral planes; psychedelics, hypnotherapy, meditation, self-help books, journaling, forums, lectures, and anything that promoted improved clarity. Basically, I was open to whatever fell upon me.

Throughout this great u n r a v e l i n g, I realized how much I was looking at the outside world for validation versus realizing my *innate wholeness*. I would put work and my writing before simple things like cooking stir-fry, separating my whites from darks (still can't seem to conquer that one), or bothering with my health. I chose to ignore my sacred vessel for the sake of worldly achievements. Some of the time, this resulted in relatively harmless pitfalls like midday naps from depleted energy or taking on a secret alter ego, Brad, the Monster Rehab brosef. Or, it led to being hospitalized for six days with a kidney infection, bloating to the heavens with fluid and morphine.

The vicious self-inflicted cycle could probably generate enough energy to power a Walmart Supercenter and single-handedly scrape off just as much of the ozone layer. I would stress myself out, douse myself in booze, spiral to the third circle of hell the next morning, oil-up my insides to fend off the nausea, punish myself and wallow in shame, work out or restrict my calories, and then enter back into the cyclical vortex. All reactionary. All bad. A debauchee's personal underworld. I avoided doing the deeper work like I stay the hell out of the DMV.

Instead of taking things in stride and putting myself first, I placed accomplishments and work before all, and consequently felt guilty if I ever prioritized my foundational well-being. If I had time to clean or cook, it meant that I wasn't doing other, "more important" things. Ironically, quality faltered in all realms because I was sprinting a marathon with knee-less Barbie legs.

When I finally prioritized my physical form and adopted new rituals, a new portal of inspiration widened. I felt replenished whenever I nourished myself with home-cooked vegan meals and consistent sessions at the gym (rather than for the purpose of counteracting my poison intake); and when I allowed both my masculine and feminine energies to blossom and merge; and when I started truly living with intention. Forgiving myself. Forgiving others.

As a self-identified tomboy, it was critical that I could balance both sides of myself, the female and male aspects of my personality. The more time I took for myself, the more energy and creative grit I could infuse into my pursuits. I could say "yes" and "no" and m e a n it, only wanting to act in my authenticity, only when I could participate fully. I stopped (or reduced greatly) judging myself and comparing myself to other women. I started seeing other women as allies, as beautiful, complex creatures who could only add to my betterment, not strip me of it. It was so freeing, being able to witness the ethereal constant within each human (and that of myself, simultaneously). Our connection to one another allowed for a pathway to self-discovery and acceptance. I was seeing our little rotating baby planet through new eyes, eyes that saw past the illusion of the physical world and into the mystical nature of the u n k n o w n.

The more time I spent nurturing myself, the more I liked it:

looking for vitamins that could suit my needs, pampering myself with bath bombs and essential oils, incorporating celery juice into my daily routine, meditating, taking walks, and finding elements of self-care that I could do religiously and with enjoyment. Also, sporadically eating a giant carne asada burrito. Keep it real, my dudes.

Being a human means enjoying the physical world, but not being trapped by it. How can we make these revolutions around the sun a little bit better for me, and for you? The more we invest in ourselves, the more our friends, colleagues, and the general population will feel open to doing the same. When we care for ourselves, we can better care for the ones around us. Otherwise, we're deteriorating ghosts attempting to conquer the world with very little progress to show for it.

Sooner or later, if you neglect yourself in exchange for business goals, relationships, or any other number of things that exist outside of you, something's gonna give. You might notice an increase in sickness, sudden injuries, unsavory moods, or an instance in which your body is telling you *lay off, lady. Let me live.*

There really is a time and a place for everything. Be patient with yourself.

When I started my business, it required significant work. Even more than I had previously anticipated. I had to make a lot of sacrifices for it, but with a long-term goal in mind. The concessions I made short-term would pay off in dividends.

Today, I can truly say that I love myself. I'm not willing to invest in relationships in which my partner doesn't fully *see* me. I'm not willing to attempt to make a relationship work when my partner is clearly not invested. I know I'm not going to be everyone's hot fuckin' cup of chamomile. Loving myself is being c h i l l with this notion. Sometimes the lack of reciprocity is meant to *show* us something. Until we finally see the endless, divine beauty of ourselves, we will continue to try to fit a circle into a square. We'll continue to have relationships that fail to please us. We'll continue to try and make someone like us, just to prove something to ourselves.

The revelations that were coming to the surface for me on a personal level then expanded, revealing my greater purpose in this life. Without the noise of the external world's demands of me, I could envision what I wanted for myself. I saw my life with greater clarity, like removing a curtain from its window. I had to give up the ghost, and that meant taking full accountability for who I was and who I wanted to become. A continuous unraveling and reshaping. And yet, remaining much of the same (at least, the good parts). The steady emergence of the soul and its conduit body.

Wholeness, I should mention, is also embracing all parts of yourself, good and bad. That means recognizing the not-so-glamorous aspects of our being. No one is (or will be) entirely good. Have this sense of acceptance for yourself and for others. We're all just trying to do this damn thang. Have patience. Life is challenge and perseverance, a continual process of reemergence. *Plunge.* Come to surface.

We will learn a lesson of transience whether it's in purview or not. Let's take the body. We are born into a precious skeletal framework, and we can either accept it or not. We can grasp onto it, attempting to capture its glory and never let go, or, we can see it as a useful, yet fleeting structure from which we can thrive. We must honor our bodies but not latch onto them. Thus, we go through life and try to stay young. We botox, we plump, we lift (and we lift, brah). But sooner or later, we will witness the degradation of this physical self. We can bemoan, or we can cherish the process, knowing that this fate is upon us and a necessary transition. (Mind you, there's nothing wrong with wanting to look good, but we must see it for what it's worth.) Even if we do not reconcile with this destiny within the earlier years of our existence, we will have to come to terms with it eventually (if even at the time of death). All things are attempting to return back to their essential nature, and such is the circular nature of the body, which eventually dies and returns back to the earth. This sacrifice of body lends itself to the release of the soul, which will remain as energy and morph into something else — that is, if you vibe with that sort of philosophy. Otherwise, even for the atheists, your body will still perish and return to its original state of oneness with nature, as all things do. All retreat to dust once more. A merging with the earth.

All of life is essentially teaching us the same lesson: the impermanence and illusory nature of the physical world. There is no objective reality, only our subjective assessment of it. Nothing is quite as it seems, and it's in our best interest to recognize this so that we can truly flourish and expand our minds and souls. To live a full life is to reach for wholeness. Wholeness of body, completion of soul, and fulfillment of p u r p o s e.

Step 39

Define your purpose.

Define your beauty.

Define what wholeness means to you.

SEEING THE FLAWS IN OTHERS / SEEING THE FLAWS IN OURSELVES

The easiest defense mechanism available to us is the divine tool belt of judgment. If everyone else orchestrates a self-deluded shitstorm with their time on this planet, and we get to be the delighted onlooker, popcorn in palm, suddenly all focus is on the other and not our own missteps. Suddenly our narrative reigns supreme and all of our fellow humans are at our selective mercy.

For myself, cynicism was (and—let's be real—still is at times) something that I held close to the clutch, like an odd and kind of off-putting calling card. I might compare it to meeting someone and, within the first three sentences of interaction, they confess to you that they love to lick golf balls. Curious. Too soon. Please leave. (There's that judgment again.) It's fine. Keep on taste-testing.

Paired with my second language of sarcasm, the two combined made for a spectacularly ambiguous sense of self. Generally, even I wouldn't truly know where the joke ended and the reality began. Sort of exhausting tbh.

I could differentiate myself from everyone and poke holes in any argument. Not to say that I have abandoned these practices entirely, but with time and awareness, it slowly dwindled down to a softer murmur. Self-made armor is the s t u r d i e s t kind.

When we are in attack mode, even in the form of mental or verbal judgment, we retreat to earlier, less evolved states of being. When I judge and negatively assess the actions and behaviors of others, I am living unconsciously. I lack g r a c e.

To notice a flaw in another is to recognize it in ourselves. The best thing to do is accept it for what it is and move on, or learn from it. Ruminate. See the m i r r o r before us.

There is a component of self-coddling present whenever we attempt to undo what another person is actively pursuing or embodying for us. We pick apart. Judge. Correct their inherent wrong. Pretend to not notice someone in a well-attended room. Toss grenades and flee from shrapnel. It's a very convenient and low-key clever way of avoiding ourselves and the work that needs to be done.

Nothing exists in a vacuum. I realized over time that my behavioral shortcomings often stemmed from events at an early age.

As someone who has struggled with the depths and nuances of sexuality since childhood, an unfortunate product of trauma, I found myself making sense of its breadth through categorization and structure. It was a coping mechanism, the only thing accessible to me that would actually ease my inner turmoil. If I could understand the "rights" and "wrongs" of the outer world, I could then properly assimilate and subsequently shed my annihilating guilt and the sharp hatred I held for myself. If I could just illustrate the perfect roadmap, I'd be golden. At least, that's hindsight speaking for the baby person I once was.

I couldn't learn to navigate the world of sexuality without first assessing it and labeling which actions were innately *good* and which were *bad*. I gathered cues from my parents, family, culture, religion, community; an ever-evolving index of right and wrong behavior. I wanted to know where I fit in. I wanted to be g o o d.

- Overt sexuality in social contexts: bad.
- Flaunting the female body: bad.
- Sex outside of a monogamous relationship: bad.
- Marriage: good.
- Chastity: great.
- Pornography: bad.
- Masturbation: bad.
- ...
- ...
- ...

Through my constant categorization, I realized that I couldn't stop with sexuality. If I really wanted to carve out a place for myself in the admissible, pure realm of humanity, I had to put the whole of the world in t i n y little boxes. What were the essential rules of morality and how could I master them?

I would pray to God and plead for his forgiveness, beg him to shed the hardened coal from my corroding soul. It was very heavy and all-consuming for years. I never thought I would reach salvation of any kind, forever stained by the penetrating darkness of shame. I wanted to dissolve my past, abandon myself. Wash away.

Guilt that festered within me from childhood held onto me into my high school years like a creeping noose. One misstep and my spirit would cave in on itself. I tried everything to distract myself. My modus operandi was to smother myself with good grades and a shining soccer reputation for the sake of gaining whatever ethical high ground was available to me. The physical world freaked me the fuck out. As I got older, the shame wilted a bit, but the pristine boxes remained. The systematic categorization of my world continued on with an automatic, nagging persistence. It filtered into everything; a safe haven laid brick by brick with moral certitude. Judgment became my essential mode of being. My second nature. I was ok there.

All of this was born of fear.

For me, making friends was always a daunting, seemingly impossible task. I didn't know how to make small talk or find a way to break the barriers of my debilitating shyness. People scared me. A room full of strangers was a recipe for a personal potluck in hell. I was a turtle in shell.

Freshman year of high school, I was the type of student who got asked to babysit for her math teacher. Despite being forced to sleep by way of pirated Lord of the Rings movies, it was a cush gig, what with the "baby" being a thirteen-year-old mama's boy with a wardrobe consisting of a single tie-dyed shirt. (Honestly, me at 13 but as the opposite gender.) Sophomore year, I was granted my out from the straight-laced existence of my youth. I was tied so tightly for so long that my eventual unwinding and inevitable plunge into the world of drugs and alcohol was really no surprise. Finally, a substance that could provide me with a little social lubricant. I fell in with a new group of friends and discovered liquid courage via alcohol, the disgusting glory of black cherry vodka, Malibu and/or Parrot Bay straight from the bottle. Eleganza! I was ripe for it, this new, improved sense of self.

The pendulum swung with an itching impatience, and I found myself experimenting with cocaine, Ecstasy/Molly, kleptomania, Oxycodone, Percocet, Lortab, Xanax, and whatever else was offered to me, whatever could allow me to levitate above body for a bit. The first time I blacked out at a party, someone found a crack pipe in my purse. I mean, I'm pretty sure I didn't smoke crack, but who's to say? This did not stop me from blacking out another 30 (an educated guess) times in the following ten years. I don't know the exact number of people I've slept with because I don't have the memory to support the count. My mind called in sick those days.

And the really cool thing about it all was that I never lost my judgmental attitude, so now I was an asshole too. Real winner, ya know?

I fostered the extreme: mobilized a genocide of my brain cells and obliterated authentic friendships and relationships in general that meant a lot to me, all at the hands of substance abuse. Nonetheless, I reasoned it away. Chalked it up to antics of the young! wild! free! Until suddenly I was puking up stomach acid in my 20s, stuffing a burger in my face to down the Excedrin. Only Excedrin, because after years of prison-grade torturous hangovers complete with seven hours of puking, I knew that migraine strength was the only thing that could get the job done with efficiency, if not a little nausea. That, plus nine baths, 15 ice cubes slathered onto my face, three cold packs, and six hours of naps and I would be back in the good graces of "health." Meaning, not death. This was the aftercare ritual. I've probably spent the same amount of time over a toilet bowl as I have in line at the grocery store.

I ate before drinking to prepare the body for the poison. I ate while and after drinking to appease the hunger gods. I ate the next day to rid myself of the pain. My life centered around alcohol and catered to it.

No offense but I'm a shitty drunk.

That isn't to say that alcohol is the devil and should be outlawed. For me, though, boundaries were merely hopeful suggestions. Drinking became at once a crutch and a curse. A frenemy, if you will.

My life took a fairly dramatic turn in high school. I was dubbed "Most Changed" in my yearbook, to qualify. Even so, I can't imagine what life I would have led if not for my rebellious streak. Would I continue on in buttoned-up perpetuity until I eventually perished in a cubicle, drowning in Bible quotes and my rare Snuggie collection? What if I only treasured the cinematic wonderment of Christian Mingle (the movie that I've never seen and never will)? Or what if something more balanced and healthy was available to me? W h a t i f.

Was the abrupt shift in the opposite direction the only inevitable future? Hard to tell from this angle, but retrospective hypotheticals do little for the complexion. Maybe some parallel universe exists where I am skipping along to Sunday School. But, you know, probably not.

Thankfully, the drug-induced psychosis of my final high school years was laid to rest (mostly, at least) when I entered college. Attending a private university away from my core group of friends catapulted me into a situation without convenient hook-ups.

My first semester of college was nothing short of a nightmare. No longer manually fueled by substances and occupying a single-person dorm room, my usual crutches were unavailable. The insecurities of my youth came showering upon me like some demented theatrical rain scene. I was tempted to transfer schools, where I could at least know a familiar face.

Until, of course, my last resort arrived: joining a sorority. *Insta-friends.* Like magic, my old pal alcohol was in the mix again. I drank and studied on the side, sort of. I partied and returned to full form.

One night I even got sent to the drunk tank, via cop car, though I have little to no recollection of the affair. To get this erased from my permanent record, I had to deliver a speech to my sorority about the do's and don'ts of public intoxication. Very classy — I'm aware. Nonetheless, I graduated and proved to everyone that I was literate by obtaining an English degree.

But yeah, what a m e s s I was. How's that for a grand reveal? We all have our demons.

The years following college, I was able to gain some clarity and focus. As my self-worth strengthened, my need to get lost in the sauce steadily declined. It wasn't the easiest or quickest route, but the destination was *well worth it*. I'd like to think that I'm exactly where I am supposed to be.

It does get better.

Step 40

There are so many possible trajectories for our lives. The point at which you are today is one of infinite realities. You may stop and ask if this is where you should be. You are always where you should be. Make the choices for you today that will allow your future self to prosper.

What boxes have you built for yourself?

How can you break them down?

INFORMAL ABSOLUTION AND DEVISING MY DREAM

As a child, I despised church. It didn't scratch the itch, ya know? As far as my little nugget mind was concerned, I got nothing out of it, aside from exasperated yawns and the deep longing to go outside and play with my hard-earned plastic McDonald's toys. Especially being raised in the Catholic faith, I found the sermons to be endlessly boring and outdated. It seemed silly to me, having to attend once a week, wear some girlish paisley ensemble (my little tomboy self loathed anything outside of my chic Pooh Bear wardrobe and overalls), and listen to an old, dusty man drone on about a passage in the New Testament. All of this would somehow make you a good person. Also the whole cannibalism thing (the consumption of Jesus Christ, our Lord in wafer form) was eerie at best. (Though the allure of drinking wine... blood?... was palpable.)

The sequence of rituals: kneeling, standing, reciting a prayer, kneeling. It was so prescriptive and mindless. Nothing r e s o n a t e d. You would say the Lord's Prayer and, really, because you've etched it into your mind over time, the words lost their essence and cascaded into a memorized sequence of sounds.

What I came to find out in my later years was that my mom and dad jointly decided to expose us (my sisters and me) to organized religion for the sake of establishing a moral foundation outside of the home. I guess they were attempting to cover their bases, in a way. My mom (a Christian) was the steadfast believer, carting my sister and me off to the holy grounds. My dad (an atheist, I discovered in adulthood) would often opt to stay home and presumably watch sports. I remember the intense amount of envy I would have for my father's position. If dad can go to hell, how come I can't?! He would keep the shtick going by joining us once in a while, but it was fairly evident that Football reigned supreme. The true s a v i o r, if there ever was one.

The interesting thing about my parents' dynamic was the distinctive influence it had on my development. On the one hand, my mom provided me with a spiritual element that always played a vital role in my perspective of the world (if even soft and in the background, at times); solely through the parental nature of my mother, every action had a moral implication. This was gifted to me in a loving, non-judgmental way. My dad, contrastingly, always lent a critical and analytical eye, calling into question nearly everything. As a consequence of their seemingly opposite stances, I paved a way for myself that was exploratory and inquisitive, but e a g e r for *depth*. Had I been exposed to only one or the other growing up, my journey would have looked very different.

At times, I swayed pretty heavily in either direction.

The idea of heaven (and how to get there) was etched into my little, impressionable mind. Right and wrong played me like a sadistic game of waterboard. My actions were more or less motivated by some faraway cubby hole in the promised land versus doing good for the sake of bettering others, or myself. Long-term goals, but entirely self-serving. It was more selfish, securing my place beyond the pearly gates through the tests of this material world.

When I was 9 or 10, I decided to go with my friend to Jesus camp. It was my first go-around with "cool," non-denominational Christianity. What started as a modest curiosity turned into a fanatical obsession within the short week. I don't recall what did it exactly, but the effect was intense and borderline extremist. Only a week in, and I was a certified Jesus freak. A Bible-thumper through and through. When I returned home, my mom was justifiably a bit creeped out as I paraded around, armed with my sweet Jesus schwag, such as a memento that emulated the Crest toothpaste logo but read "Christ" instead, and other such hyper-clever mechanisms for kiddy conversion. Thankfully, the intensity wore off with time.

I say "thankfully" not because anything is wrong with Jesus or praising his name (Catholicism presented the same Jesus after all, if not a little more bland), but the error comes with an unhealthy attachment to any one belief system. Had I continued on in this way, I don't know that I would have had the opportunity or interest to question my beliefs.

Why Jesus? Why Christianity? Why this structure? These prayers?

In simple terms: if you eat sushi regularly because it is your favorite food, but you haven't (for some god-forsaken reason) ever tried ice cream, then maybe your relationship with sushi is conditional. Maybe your favorite food is actually ice cream, but you haven't yet experienced its otherworldly splendor. Maybe, even, upon devouring your first, single-sitting pint of culinary mastery, you decide that ice cream and sushi are both exceptional works of art. Neither is better than the other; they share a pedestal of everlasting grace and glory. The same feeling of intense joy arises from the consumption of ice cream and, to the same degree, from the sushi.

And though I am very well aware of the aspect of some organized religions (Catholicism at least) that pledges a position of belief over reason or evidence, a healthy dose of critical thinking is necessary in strengthening any belief structure. After all, if you are literally conditioned from birth to believe in one thing, the subsequent belief in that thing is no longer c h o i c e; it's merely a consequence of nurturing in a singular direction. If questioning takes place and you settle on the belief, that belief is that much stronger, having faced its obstacle of human interference. Kind of like how you don't know what happiness is without its counter: sadness. Limiting the expansiveness of divinity to a singular term, system, or book is to *diminish* it.

Now, I must say here that I have nothing against anyone's particular faith. All routes to salvation, in whatever forms they happen to occupy, are worthy of embracing for the time that they serve you. If that time happens to be a few years, so be it. A lifetime? The more the merrier. Salvation, for my purposes, is freedom in this life — allowing yourself to f e e l and b r e a t h e and ride this damn thing. Get up in the morning and look yourself in the mirror. Not hate it. Love it with every fiber within you. That is salvation. Not something that we need to decode from the annals of biblical history. Not something that comes to us like a flesh-slicing flail. Not torment and fatigue.

My zig-zagged pathway to an informal absolution (mostly granted to myself, with notable mentions being my family and close friends) began with my split from the Catholic Church.

I stuck with it throughout my earlier teens, even if my participation at that point was more obligatory, with the dark stains of the Church's outed reputation keeping me at arm's length. To be freed from guilt only through the medium of a priest in a phone booth struck me as odd and ritualistic for the sake of sustaining human ego. The same priests, marinating in their sexual repression, could then harm children? This is the state of affairs? This is the jubilant parade to the heavenly corridor?

Surely, every human on earth could be granted salvation. Why just the *Americans*? Why just the *Christians*? Or *Catholics*? Why just the *white people*? Or those who could afford to hand over their savings to add to the gold-laden altars, the hyperbolic crucified Jesus reigning over us in grand opulence? The reliance on only one faith seemed to me to be a hegemonic affair, serving to oppress all others who dare think about their time in this world in any differentiating way. Whilst, in true ironic fashion, those seemingly opposing religions were praising the same God who happened to drape a different cloak.

When I consider the big daddy book, the Bible, in my understanding of this life and our earthling relationships, I often wonder if it is the case that we're clinging to advice that is far removed from the original, intended message. That, or maybe we're not taking into consideration the chain of command leading us to a distinct passage that is, in many ways, probably obscured.

We're talking about a book from thousands of years ago; one that has been translated umpteen times, interpreted through the eyes and lips of many, many strange men, uttered to many audiences, and given to us in tiny snippets with an accompanying message that may or may not truly capture the e s s e n c e of the word. We often rely on the messenger to deliver the truth. If a single sentence in our current framework can be misconstrued in a number of ways, think about the possibility of something that was not only in an entirely different language, but likely possessed infinite connotations.

I mentioned earlier that the books of Matthew, Mark, Luke, and John were written over 40 years after the death of Jesus. Can you remember what you ate for breakfast two months ago? Sometimes I can't recall if I brushed my teeth that morning and have to check the bristles for dampness. Despite some of the misalignments when it comes to the Bible versus historical fact, I can't deny my appreciation for many of the messages within it (perhaps more allegorical than indicative of accuracy in physical time and space).

Again, I take the word and look beyond it. What can I gain from the scripture? How can I use it for the betterment of myself? Of society? Of the environment?

If I were to grasp so tightly to the language of the Bible, I couldn't merely push some passages aside, could I? Hand-pick from the greatest book that we-ever-did-see? After all, the Bible talks about servants and masters, and we all seem diametrically opposed to that notion these days... I hope. Lest we forget how fucked up the Bible once was.

We forget about the times that the Bible was altered for the sake of the king, for cardinal power; the vengeful, angry God of the Old Testament. We might ask how this body of work speaks to the age of when it was written, and how might it be applied today. Should we start owning humans again? Should women merely succumb to the masterful power of their husbands? Should men marry the women they rape?

Every written work is emblematic of its t i m e: the language, symbolism, characters, power structure, and conflicts. When we rip this work from its historical resting place, we run the risk of bastardization. Filter through filter, we muddle the words and attempt to fill a new narrative. Yes, ideas may hover over us for any length of time: love, forgive-ness, grace, and all of the constants apply to any generation. The stories display a prototype, but we are fools if we neglect to see the bigger picture and instead analyze each individual vowel and consonant for a literal translation that only con-fuses and betrays the central function of the work.

Progressive Revelation is the Christian doctrine proposing that God's essential truth was revealed in layers over the span of the Bible. More or less, God spoon-fed revelations to the people versus smacking them with it all at once; a staggering of information, if you will, so that — I would sus-pect — their heads didn't all explode. Many people point to the stark difference of the Old Testament God compared to the stevia-drunk God of the New Testament.

If you're willing to extrapolate with me a bit, this reasoning could be applied to our evolution as a species. Even in viewing works like the Bible and Quran, it would have been entirely useless bringing up gay rights back when humans were very much still in the closet. Gay people (and bi and so forth) aren't suddenly multiplying these days; we've always been complex creatures, even if social norms haven't recognized that or allowed for people to explore their sexual nature in the way that we do now, and inevitably the way we will going forward. The people of that time weren't ready for that sort of information to emerge. The Bible of today would certainly include such things, but any mention of it thousands of years ago would have amounted to a laugh track on cobblestone streets.

So, when those who claim to hold the Lord in such high esteem simultaneously ostracize their gay neighbors, is this really what the dude up top wanted? Nahhhh, most definitely not. Anything outside of love and forgiveness is not Truth.

I hear time and time again *THE BIBLE SAYS A MAN AND A WOMAN, NOT ANYTHING ELSE*. Well, yeah! That was what was culturally acceptable back then. Those words were speaking directly to the people of that time and what they were ready to hear. Of course that's what it said.

A similar circumstance occurs within our current political climate and the prevalent talking points concerning the Constitution. Is the right to bear arms (2nd Amendment) from 1791 the same as the right to bear arms in 2020? Over

200 years later? Could the people of the 18th century really foresee a single person having the ability to purchase twenty semi-automatic machine guns and kill 58 people from a hotel window? The killing machines of the past are a far cry from those of the present. Is this the gruesome freedom of expression and "protection" that we're supposed to get behind?

I d i g r e s s.

We, as a collective group, evolve over time. Ideas and theories stay in flux, and we're no exception. We're meant to *combine* and *change*, influence each other and emerge as whole beings. The growing pursuit of travel and the subsequent melding of cultures is the way in which our independent knowledge bases infuse into the overarching landscape. Our global identity is at once stratified and wholly integrated. Not only does one country influence another, but each individual person plays a part in the worldwide arena, even if that participation seems like a drop in the bucket. Every single individual is an actor in this theater.

Everything in our perceivable world, and outside of that field of understanding, is energy. We are energy. Our thoughts are e n e r g y. Everything in the physical world is made of E N E R G Y. We are constantly interacting in this magnetic push and pull of vibration. Meaning, every second, you're a participant in the great sphere of undulation. The glory! Every thought you have, whether good bad or indifferent, comes with a specific frequency, which operates much like a signal. What are you projecting? Are you aware of what you're sending out to the universe?

The more present we are, the more we can regulate and finesse our output.

We often talk about the ability to manifest. We want a new car, or a new job. We want a hot brunette who is wholeheartedly confident and somehow unabashedly humble. We want it all! But what are we manifesting each and every second? What is continually pulsating out into the ether?

Whether we want to be reflective and take accountability for our true presence in the world, we are manifesting. Always, forevermore. We're allowing ourselves to be happy, or stubborn messes carting our baggage around for everyone to see and experience. We're saviors or beggars. Nothing goes unseen. We will either throw in the towel or decide to look at each day like a singing pop-up card from Nirvana (the place or the band... pick your poison). But it's our choice. We are the o n l y ones who can decide.

Maybe our greatest contribution is a tenderness toward life? A gallant happiness and a tendency to see the silver lining? Could that be enough?

We're always, already whole. It's up to us to see and cherish the lightness that glimmers each passing moment. Embrace the Now and what the world is already giving us. The sunshine. The smell of freshly cut grass. The running water. Our working limbs. The air that makes it to our noses, mouths, and lungs. There's so much to see, appreciate, and ingest.

In 2010, I took a five-month trip to India, Nepal, and Thailand for the purpose of meditation, organic farming, and exploring the world. I guess you could say that I was ready to uproot the unsavory parts of myself in exchange for some peace of mind. The idea for my cocktail bar, Velveteen Rabbit, came to me at the beginning of the trip as I was meditating in McLeod Ganj, India in the foothills of the Himalayas. Inspiring, well-traveled visitors, paired with the serene, cloud-rich atmosphere, and my personal escape from orthodox social norms made for an environment ripe for invention. As the months progressed, the idea for the bar became more of a possible reality in my mind. The common guidelines were discarded and I could cut and paste as I pleased. The idea was to open this bar, which would be a community-driven space dedicated to art, music, and cocktails; work for myself; and write on the side for the sake of expression and purpose.

If you ever want to shake up what you regularly accept and know about the world, or yourself, go to a country on the other side of the world. I guarantee new p e r s p e c t i v e.

We possess armor of certainty — unfailing, divine intuition that ripples underneath the surface, and wants nothing more than to be cherished and celebrated. Pick up the phone, girl! Grab that receiver and dial in, because *this is your life right here*. This is your chance to do whatever the fuck it is that you want to do.

Hey, you? You're the conductor of this thing. There aren't any rules here. Yes, I mean, people will tell you there are, but you're the master of your own life. Choose your own GD adventure, ya dig?

You're 50 and want to pursue your law degree? Do it, dude.

You're a doctor and want to B-line to the hospitality industry, start your own paleo food truck? Do it!

Wanna be an artist? By all means.

Write a book? You can do it.

Love yourself and h o n o r your desires. Pick yourself up and try. Try again. Switch directions and try a little more. No matter what, no matter where you are, what you've done, where you're going, who you're going with, or what you wanna be, you must try. Look within, trust yourself, and follow your gut. Don't let the world mess with your business. Set the rules straight.

Listen up. If I did it, *so can you.*

When I was traveling abroad, my main objective was to find myself. Get out of my comfort zone. I know it's cheesy right, but what are we all doing right this moment? We're always attempting to peel the layers, aren't we? Cry, peel the onion, cry some more. Eat a nice, warm dinner. Repeat.

When I was on my fifth month of my adventure abroad after college, I was in Thailand attending the most rigorous meditation retreat of my life at a Vipassana center in Chiang Mai, Thailand: ten hours of meditation a day, 4 a.m. wake time, no eating past noon, no speaking, and no eye contact. Despite wanting to rip my hair out at hour nine each day, the silence and internal reflection allowed for a renewed clarity. You witness yourself, your voice, your chatter, without obstruction.

My time there presented me with a truth: all of our fears, anxieties, hopes, and mental blocks are of our own making.

I am my only enemy. All of my suffering is self-inflicted.

Stories from my past played on a loop, begging me to relive each memory and reconstruct the scene, the actors, the dialogue until I arrived at a pleasing scenario, only to revert back to the present, where all retellings were completely irrelevant. Rehashing the past will do nothing but steal away the present moment. You can never go back and redo what has been executed, so why relive and relive again? Learn the lesson and move on.

How often am I living in this fictionalized world? How much time am I wasting on fantasy scenarios?

I woke up to myself. I shed the heaviness of what could have been, what isn't. And with that, possibility opened up for me like the window to fall on the first day of October. It was crisp, fresh, a l i v e.

After the ten days, I was ready to fulfill my objective. I wrote an email to my sister, outlining my goal for us to open a cocktail bar, and she was taken by the concept. Velveteen Rabbit: plush Victorian furniture, seasonal craft cocktails, dim lighting. Nearly everything illustrated within that initial pitch to my sister manifested in physical form (sans food served on banana leaves, which wasn't exactly a deal breaker for either of us). As soon as my sister was on board, I grabbed a flight home to Las Vegas, moved in with my parents, and started saving money.

Age and experience were obvious concerns. At 23, you're a clueless noob in a male-dominated sphere overrun by single-barrel whiskey dilettantes and in-house bitters up to your handlebar mustache. You're still nursing vodka presses and (baby Jesus, forgive) some blue-stained drink, feigning an ounce of sophistication, while your bank account levitates right above $40. You're the tween of the drinking world. Dora the paycheck-to-paycheck explorer.

I couldn't even name four wine varietals without mentioning White Zin.

Thankfully for me, I was so ridiculously naive that I didn't think the endeavor would be that hard a task.

How hard could it be? Cities are brimming with bars.

Seeing as I had never managed a bar, much less bartended in one, my knowledge base was flapjack thin. I knew I was smart-ish, with an incredible drive when necessary, and that was basically all I had in my arsenal. I had maintained various positions within restaurants for the ten years prior, but nothing in the way of actually operating a business.

Doors opened for us, despite taking two-and-a-half years after conception to actualize the dream. At the time, the city government was attempting to revitalize the Arts District of Las Vegas, providing grants and free liquor licenses to potential business owners who would dare open doors on Main Street, which needed a lot of love. We took advantage of all monetary help available, built an extensive home bar, researched, studied, thwarted off nay-sayers, and crossed a lot of fingers.

Was everyone spellbound by my intense passion to live out my dream?! Oh, HELL NO. The amount of people who shat on my parade was, well... let's just say I didn't receive the resounding applause I was hoping for. Most people thought we were insane, dumb, foolish, inexperienced, or a sweet combo. We had to be our own cheerleaders for a lot of that time, alongside the support from our parents.

I worked as a server for those two-and-a-half years because no one would hire me as a bartender.

You have to b e l i e v e in *yourself* when no one else does.

Within the first couple of years of opening, we put our heads down and worked non-stop 80-hour weeks, making a name for ourselves and trying not to go completely mental in the process. We wore many hats: bartender, manager, owner, friend, foe. Within the first year, we were named in the top 50 for up-and-coming faces in the industry nation-wide. In the years following, we were featured in *Esquire, New York Times, Wall Street Journal, Nylon, Bon Appetit, Paste, Playboy, Vice, Imbibe, LA Times,* and *Forbes.* We won awards like Best Cocktail Menu, Best Locals Bar, and Cocktail Bar of the Year.

It was a trip. It exceeded anything we could have imagined.

I ended up opening the bar when I was 25, and I found myself dodging questions about my background or know-how. After we were a few years in, I was more comfortable sharing my lack of expertise upon opening, but I knew that if I was open about my novice status at the beginning, people would be less impressed and more inquisitive. If you don't abide by the regulated way of doing things, you're automatically set up to fail, at least in the eyes of the others. People don't want to see their tried-and-true structures crumble before them. If this, then what else? People like the tiny little boxes with the structure and false sense of comfort they hold, however flimsy.

If you have a dream, you have to be willing to sacrifice greatly for it. For us, that meant neglecting a lot of our close relationships for the sake of the business, spending 16-hour days on our feet, and basically living at the bar. The freedom that I now have with my business is such a welcome reward after years of long, late nights, criticism from those who thought we were too green to have a place at the table, and attempting to figure out all of the programming and operations that were so foreign to us prior to opening.

Owning a restaurant was something that appealed to me from a very early age; when I realized that, as an adult human being, I could still hardly cook an egg, my interest switched to bars. Conceptualizing different establishments was something I found myself doing quite often. In my mind, though, I settled on the fact that if I were to ever own a bar, it would have to be later in life, per societal recommendations (subtle or not). To think of doing it earlier seemed unrealistic or perhaps even selfish. *Who am I to think that I can figure something out and make it a success?*

Having spent some time in college writing for a local San Diego magazine, it was clear to me that if I wanted to solely pursue writing, I might have to craft it in such a way to either A. appease my editor or B. appease some audience that may or may not be my own. For me, the goal would be to write whatever I wanted without the need to be financially supported by it. The absolute fantasy would be to combine the two goals together: open an establishment and become an author.

It took me a minute, sure. After opening the bar in 2013, it took another seven years to get to the place I am today, where we now have a manager and I do not have to be physically present as much as I once was.

I am not exaggerating when I say that I live the life that I once only d r e a m e d about. Parts of it weren't fun, and I wanted to abandon ship at certain points, but ultimately, I stayed true to myself and what I wanted.

Now, this dream isn't for everyone. Your aspiration might be traveling, or eating hot dogs for a living. Maybe it's becoming a veterinarian. Maybe it's skydiving or being a goddamn calligrapher. Who knows! The thing is, we're all such complex and versatile creatures. If you look within and honor what you were given, you can find a way to incorporate it into your life and the world around you with a finesse and style that is *all your own*. Maybe you don't know what it is right now. Maybe you know one small sliver of it. It's all good! Take that piece and see where it takes you. Be open to exploring the various aspects of yourself and your innate abilities.

At certain points leading up to our opening, I would share my vision with my peers. My goals looked unattainable and downright Britney Spears circa 2007 in their eyes. Most people would give the expected "oh, that's nice" response, eyes dead and bulging with apathy. Other people would laugh, humored by our impending failure. It got to the point where we would stop talking about it with others. No one believed us. It didn't matter. Sometimes being the clear outsider is a g o o d thing. You're veering from the pack and constructing your own destiny in the way you see fit. In any case, when people do not share your vision or encourage you in the way you'd like, it's not always a bad thing. You're being tested. How much do you want this? What are you willing to sacrifice for your inherent destiny? Trust your gut and make it happen, baby! No one's gonna do it for ya.

Here's the thing with dreams: it's only your responsibility to believe in them.

Had I listened to all of the cynics, the dream would have never come to fruition. If what you do is abide by the standards of everyone else, you've gone a s t r a y.

That doesn't mean that you shouldn't always consider the advice of others, especially if you trust those people. Sometimes constructive criticism kicks you in the ass and also tells you something kinda useful. Take it. Other times, you politely listen and then, suitably, politely decline. It's up to you to discern.

Head above that salty sea. Listen to that intuition and keep your wits about you.

If you haven't figured it out by now, I'm really not preaching anything new. We're all piggy-backing on the information given to us since birth. Pick and choose. And be selective. It's your life. You live it.

Remember, we're all *making it up*.

We have a duty to be boundless and authentic, to pay homage to the little child inside of you that aches to be seen for who you truly are. Not the conformist. Not the spectator. But the champion of hope and the possibility for positive evolution. The evolution of you, of your soul, and of the collective body.

Fear ain't anything but a story, bb. Do you and do it right. Don't overthink the complexities of your growth and where you're going. Each day, take a little step. Then another step forward. Sooner or later, you'll get there, wherever *there* is for you.

When I conceived of my brainchild, I went forward with pure force, a force that could not be dampened by the salty opinions of those around me. That was nearly ten years ago and what am I doing now? Living out my goddamn truth, girl! It's real! And the only thing I may have missed? That I didn't dream *big* enough! I'm at my destination, and now I have to scoot up to the drawing board and dream up a few more things. That's the beauty of it all: it never ends. Not while you've got breath to give.

10, 20, 30, 80, 90… you're still livin', you've still got something left. Make it up as you go, sketch out the lines, and color it in, but never say it's too late. Never succumb to the social norms.

What would I do now if I listened to all of those loud-as-hell voices? Well, I'd be a sore loser of life.

32, no children, with a giant rabbit babygirl named Steve. These aren't necessarily the markers of a good life according to the masses.

But what are my personal goals?

Happiness, financial security, good friends, lots of good food and drink. May these options fluctuate to fit my life at a later date? Sure, but that's for me to decide.

I work for myself, do as I please, spend time with my friends, travel the world, and write to my heart's content. Maybe for you, this isn't the story of success. Well, it's a good thing I'm not you, huh?!

As a very wise philosopher once spoke: *haters gon' hate.* Everyone will have an opinion. If your objective is to be liked by everyone, then I'm sorry to report that you are going to proceed with very little success. The more work you do, the larger the opportunity for haters to multiply, combine, and attempt to ruffle those voluptuous feathers of yours.

Two rules for going forward:

1. Death is inevitable
2. Haters gon' hate

That was a bit of a sardonic approach, but let's be real: not everyone is going to get you, and it's not their responsibility to understand your objectives. It's all good, dude! Live anyway.

Haters gon' hate. Live anyway.

People will judge. Live anyway.

Life comes with hurdles. Live anyway.

Here's the thing, if you're living the safe life, you're not challenging yourself. Growth comes with some pains, but it's like that soreness that washes over you after a hard workout: shows that you got it done, kicked some ass, and took some names (metaphorically?).

And the thing is, even if you're taking risks or chilling in the back, life is still going to hand you some challenges anyway. Life's basically saying, *Duuuuuude, wake your ass up! Pay attention.*

Life doesn't have to be an uninspired, live-like-you're-dying sequence of events. Alternatively, maybe that's what you want. That's fine too. Live fully! Live often! Live as you see fit.

Now, the minor downfall of all of this is that you're going to have to make some sacrifices along the way. The first of which is being unapologetically you.

You are a d i a m o n d, my friend. Act like it.

By this, I don't mean that you now have a hall pass to act like an asshole and say that you're "being real." My goodness, eye rolls aplenty. No. What I mean is: dig deep and find out what it is that you're here for. How can you express yourself in full color? How can you contribute to the whole in an expressive, lasting way? You know what it is. Don't you?

We've created rules for ourselves, or other people have; what we need to truly embrace and absorb is the possibility of dissecting, undoing, or reassessing these restrictions on ourselves. The manner in which we have led our lives has perhaps been useful in certain ways, but in what ways has it caused us harm? Maybe even in ways beyond our understanding. Not only this, but the foundation of creating such a map for life is often times built upon fear, escape, and the alleviation of pain, if only momentarily. Is there a way to construct a map that brings about hope and love? Does it have to be this unsettling maze of defeat and fear-avoidance? What's so fucking scary, guys? The dude who won't tell you you're pretty? The job that might not hire you?

Anyone with a modicum of success will tell you that the failures teach way more than the wins, so let's learn the lessons and move forward.

Step 41

Take what works and discard the rest.

When you were dumped for the first time and your heart bled right out, did you decide enough is enough/done with this game? No, right? At least, not forever. Each failed attempt teaches us something new. If we don't learn our lesson, we will encounter this same problematic scenario over and over, indefinitely, marinating in existential dread until we do learn it. Then, inevitably, the newest edition will show up. Life is about growth, and we can only be the best me through the challenges. Embracing the challenges. Eating them right up.

Step 42
Abandon your...

EXISTENTIAL D R E A D

Nice to find you here.

In the event of possible disorientation following the previous however-many pages, let me go ahead and remind you that we (that is, you and I) have managed to navigate the treacherous battleground between the abstract, conceptual cloudthings that hang like a delicate veil overhead, and the tangible, earthly matter shrouded in the familiar density of our physical plane. The opposing force remains unknown, or perhaps missing, like shadow-cast silhouette etched on the side of a milk carton.

Or perhaps, accosted with this maddening absence of enemy, we wade in the nothingness—the heavy, penetrating silence of a moment's ceaseless returning—and only then are we able to witness the true adversary. O u r s e l v e s.

Existential dread seeps in like a stratus sheet, its creamy-grey membrane reminding us of our confined timelines, the pulsating ticktock of humanity's condition. Despite our clever tactics for distraction and camouflage, the rhythmic haunt persists. A ghostly cadence of our inevitable finality. The ice cream's slow melt.

In the presence of this fate, two choices remain: continue on in foggy slumber, dulling the vibrancy of our energetic core. or. awaken our senses, *our self*, to the rich fluidity of life, oscillating between ethereal splendor and the interconnected nature of our material corridor.

ACKNOWLEDGMENTS

This definitely isn't a one-man show, and I owe mountains of thanks and gratitude to some tremendously supportive people in my life. Without them, this book would be nonexistent. And in the case of my parents, I myself would be nonexistent, so there's that.

Speaking of which: Mom and dad, you both have encouraged me to wander and search for my personal freedom and self-expression in whatever ways spoke to me throughout the years. Even if that meant bowling lessons at six-years-old or buying a hearse at 32. You created structure but allowed for exploration, and others aren't always so blessed with a solid home or familial environment, so thank you. And a trillion other thank yous, but my space is limited in this format.

To Pam: We're in this thing together, and I cherish the bond we've cultivated along the way. You are my sister, my friend, my business partner. Wonderful weirdos. Thank you for being unapologetically you and allowing me to do the same.

Tanya: Thank you for always bolstering my confidence through the praise of my writing abilities and generous excitement for each new project or idea. It has meant more than you know, especially when my self-assurance was severely lacking.

Diane: Thank you for acting as the catalyst for transformation and reconciliation in our family (and beyond); your purpose serves my purpose, and this book is a direct result.

To the rest of my extended family: Your perseverance and strength of character know no bounds. You've set the standard. Thank you.

Megan: Your brilliance inspires me, and this work would be a garbled mess if it weren't for your editorial guidance. Thank you for that, and thank you for being nice about it.

Chels: Thank you for the sacrifice of your time for my own branding purposes (read also: gain). Your creativity is in a constant state of flow, and I'm grateful that it flooded into my realm of things.

Billy: Your magnetic energy cannot be contained. Thank you for the late-night chats and the reminders to embrace full potential.

To Davey (and the staff): Beyond thankful for your hard work and consistent dedication to the vision of Velveteen Rabbit. Without you, I wouldn't be able to pursue other passions (i.e., this.).

Mallory: Thank you for always being my hype(wo)man in the wings and opening my virgin eyes to experiential design.

Ani: Your drive keeps me humble. Thank you for being so open and accepting of me.

To Hanna and my moon people: Thank you for assisting in the manifestation of this dream.

Wizard: Thank you for nurturing all of my weird.

BT: Yeah, man. Thanks for exploring the other realms with me and delighting in my innate absurdity.

Bri guy: Everyone needs a personal cheerleader. Thank you for that. When in doubt, drink more water.

Thank you to my Scribe publishing team for the seamless process, the on-point design work, and the enjoyable collaboration.

Thank you to ice cream, my muse.

Thank you to Oprah, my queen.

And thank you to you, for reading.

Made in the USA
Middletown, DE
13 May 2020